GLOBALIZATION AND MEDIA

Global Village of Babel

JACK LULE

ROWMAN & LITTLEFIELD PUBLISHERS, INC.
Lanham • Boulder • New York • Toronto • Plymouth, UK

Published by Rowman & Littlefield Publishers, Inc.
A wholly owned subsidiary of The Rowman & Littlefield Publishing Group, Inc.
4501 Forbes Boulevard, Suite 200, Lanham, Maryland 20706
www.rowmanlittlefield.com

Estover Road, Plymouth PL6 7PY, United Kingdom

British Library Cataloguing in Publication Information Available

Library of Congress Cataloging-in-Publication Data

Lule, Jack, 1954–
    Globalization and media : global village of Babel / Jack Lule.
       p. cm. — (Globalization)
    Includes bibliographical references and index.
    ISBN 978-0-7425-6835-8 (cloth : alk. paper) — ISBN 978-0-7425-6836-5
(pbk. : alk. paper) — ISBN 978-0-7425-6837-2 (electronic : alk. paper)
    1. Mass media and globalization.   2. Culture and globalization.   I. Title.
    P94.6.L845 2011
    302.23—dc23   2011032442

♾ ™ The paper used in this publication meets the minimum requirements of
American National Standard for Information Sciences—Permanence of Paper for
Printed Library Materials, ANSI/NISO Z39.48-1992.

Printed in the United States of America

GLOBALIZATION

Series Editors

Manfred B. Steger

Royal Melbourne Institute of Technology and University of Hawai'i–Mānoa

and

Terrell Carver

University of Bristol

"Globalization" has become *the* buzzword of our time. But what does it mean? Rather than forcing a complicated social phenomenon into a single analytical framework, this series seeks to present globalization as a multidimensional process constituted by complex, often contradictory interactions of global, regional, and local aspects of social life. Since conventional disciplinary borders and lines of demarcation are losing their old rationales in a globalizing world, authors in this series apply an interdisciplinary framework to the study of globalization. In short, the main purpose and objective of this series is to support subject-specific inquiries into the dynamics and effects of contemporary globalization and its varying impacts across, between, and within societies.

Globalization and Sovereignty
John Agnew

Globalization and War
Tarak Barkawi

Globalization and Human Security
Paul Battersby and Joseph
M. Siracusa

Globalization and American Popular Culture, Second Edition
Lane Crothers

Globalization and Militarism
Cynthia Enloe

Globalization and Law
Adam Gearey

Globalization and Feminist Activism
Mary E. Hawkesworth

Globalization and Postcolonialism
Sankaran Krishna

Globalization and Media
Jack Lule

Globalization and Social Movements
Valentine Moghadam

Globalization and Terrorism, Second Edition
Jamal R. Nassar

Globalization and Culture, Second Edition
Jan Nederveen Pieterse

Globalization and International Political Economy
Mark Rupert and M. Scott Solomon

Globalization and Islamism
Nevzat Soguk

Globalisms, Third Edition
Manfred B. Steger

Rethinking Globalism
Edited by Manfred B. Steger

Globalization and Labor
Dimitris Stevis and Terry Boswell

Globaloney 2.0
Michael Veseth

Supported by the Globalization Research Center at the University of Hawai'i–Mānoa

CONTENTS

PREFACE

"Dad," my eighteen-year-old son asks, "what's your book about?" "Globalization and media," I tell him. He looks at me for a long while. "Dad," he says. "I don't even know what those words mean."

Here is his typical day: He wakes to a blaring clock radio and lies in bed until he hears the weather report. He showers while listening to his iPod, which was made in Taiwan and assembled and shipped from Shanghai. He eats breakfast while watching SportsCenter and reading the sports pages. He checks his cell phone for messages. He drives to school in his Honda, likely made in the United Kingdom and Japan, with the radio on, passing flashing billboards that advertise cars made in Germany and sneakers made in South Korea. He attends school, in some classes using a Macintosh produced in Shanghai and in other classes watching foreign films. He eats lunch with two friends. One friend is Dominican and Puerto Rican. The other friend's parents emigrated from Ghana to the United States. After school, my son returns home and sits down at the computer to finish his homework. After dinner, perhaps Chinese or Mexican food, if homework is finished he repairs to the basement and goes online to play video games such as *Call of Duty*, battling others logged on from around the world, while also chatting on the phone and keeping an eye on the television. He goes to bed with the iPod playing softly beside him.

Globalization and media are embedded in almost every aspect of his daily existence. Yet he does not know what the words mean. I don't fault my son at all. The terms are difficult and vague. They mean everything and nothing. And economic, political, and cultural debates have served further to complicate them. Yet globalization and media are simply modern terms for things people have been doing for a very long time. And they will shape my son's world for years to come.

I have taught classes in international communication, mass communication, media and society, and global studies for more than twenty years. In that time and in those classes, I have tried to pull together the people, events, concepts, and theories that shape the world of my students. I have tried to share them in this book. I have come to believe that few forces are more powerful in this world than globalization and media. This book is an attempt at understanding what those words mean.

ACKNOWLEDGMENTS

Books result from professional and personal support.

Professionally, my support for this book has come first from Lehigh University. I hold dual positions in global studies and journalism and communication. It is thus little wonder that I produced a book on globalization and media. Faculty and students have contributed much to this work. My students will recognize the people and ideas in the pages that follow. Still, I likely would not have pursued a book on globalization and media without an invitation from Manfred Steger. He and Terrell Carver are editors of the Globalization series for Rowman and Littlefield. Their support, and the support of Susan McEachern, editorial director, has been invaluable.

Personally, my support for this book has come from family and friends. My mother and father long ago encouraged me to travel and write. Decades later, I still travel and write. My wife, Gregorie, and three sons, John, Nick and Joe, often must endure a husband and father who spends too much time hunched over a laptop computer. Their love and support helped shape this book. Their love and support also help shape my full and happy hours.

1

INTRODUCTION

Global Village of Babel

The new electronic interdependence recreates the world in the image of a global village.

—Marshall McLuhan

Therefore its name was called Babel, because there the Lord confused the language of the whole earth; and from there the Lord scattered them abroad over the face of the whole earth.

—Genesis 11:9

WAEL GHONIM

Wael Ghonim, thirty, was the head of marketing for Google in the Middle East and North Africa. Born in Cairo, he earned a computer engineering degree and MBA there. He brought to Google strengths in computer technology, business, marketing, and communication. He was on a fast track to success at the company. In January 2011, the people of Tunisia in northern Africa overthrew their dictator. Cairo, too, was stirring with talk of protest. Egypt had endured thirty years of brutal dictatorship under Hosni Mubarak. Ghonim took a leave of absence from Google.

Months before, unknown to Google, Ghonim had secretly put in motion a social media campaign that was galvanizing and inspiring the Egyptian people. Ghonim had created a Facebook page, "We Are All Khaled Said," which portrayed and protested the death of a twenty-eight-year-old man beaten to death in 2010 by Egyptian police. The page showed horrific cell phone photographs of Khaled Said's tortured body. Links to YouTube photographs and videos dramatized the death even more. Other abuses were reported and recorded on the page. The site attracted immense interest throughout Egypt. Human rights groups, social justice movements, and others too began using the Facebook page as well as Twitter and other media to inform Egyptians, especially young people, about police abuse and other issues. Demonstrations were discussed. On January 25, a massive rally at Tahrir Square in Cairo surprised authorities. Revolution was in the air.[1]

On January 28, 2011, Ghonim disappeared. It was widely believed that Egyptian police had learned of his social media campaign and seized him. Google, Amnesty International, and other groups called for his release. Demonstrations continued to be held at Tahrir Square. On February 7, 2011, twelve days after his disappearance, Ghonim was released. Just two hours later, he appeared on national television. In an intense, emotional interview, he described his captivity, mourned protesters who had been killed, and called for the end of the Mubarak regime. Two days later, he stepped on stage and rallied the huge crowd at Tahrir Square.

Observing events, one scholar noted, "No turbaned ayatollah had stepped forth to summon the crowd. This was not Iran in 1979. A young Google executive, Wael Ghonim, had energized this protest when it might have lost heart."[2] Ghonim had become "the symbol of Egypt's revolution."[3] Ghonim himself downplayed his role. He told the crowd at Tahrir Square, "This is not the time for individuals, or parties, or movements. It's a time for all of us to say just one thing: Egypt above all."[4] Two days later, on February 11, 2011, Hosni Mubarak stepped down as president of Egypt.

Ghonim told an interviewer, "I want to meet Mark Zuckerberg [Facebook's founder] one day and thank him. This revolution started online. This revolution started on Facebook."[5]

MARTIN LUTHER

Martin Luther was a German professor and priest in the Roman Catholic Church. In the early 1500s, Luther became disenchanted with his church. At the time, the Church said people could buy "indulgences" to rid themselves of sins. Luther believed that forgiveness of sins was a gift of God that could not be purchased. He was enraged that the Church would violate the central principles of penance and contrition. In 1517, he wrote down his argument. Legend says he nailed his argument—his Ninety-Five Theses—to the door of the Castle Church in Wittenberg, Germany. This may have happened. But there is no doubt what did happen.

The printing press had come to Europe in 1450. Luther recognized the power of this still-new medium.[6] He first oversaw the translation of the theses from Latin, the language of the Church, to German, the language of the people. He then oversaw the mass printing and distribution of the theses. The book was translated into English, French, and Italian and circulated throughout Europe. His actions with the Wittenberg church, which would have been a local dispute, became an international confrontation that rocked all of Europe. One scholar noted, "Efforts by the church to suppress Luther's writings were fruitless. Too many presses, too many booksellers, and too many trade routes made it impossible for the church to prevent the dissemination of printed matter it opposed."[7]

Luther pressed his advantage. He continued to write. He published books and pamphlets. He was the best-selling author of his generation. He advocated more reliance on the Bible, especially when Catholic teaching deviated from the Bible. He rejected the rich, corrupt, and worldly ways of the Catholic hierarchy. People throughout Europe began celebrating "Lutheran" services. The services were understood as protests of Roman Catholic practice and came to be known as "Protestant." Religion was never to be the same.

Yet Luther's use of the printing press had impacts far outside religion. The repudiation of papal authority led to the decline of the power of the Church over Europe. With this decline, nations and states arose. As the Church's sway over buying, selling, and consumption lessened, commercialism expanded. In February 1546, Luther died. He had used the printing press to transform his world.[8]

OPRAH WINFREY

Her story has inspired women worldwide. Oprah Winfrey was born in rural Mississippi in 1954 to unmarried teenagers. She was named Orpah after a Bible character in the Book of Ruth, but family and friends pronounced it "Oprah." Her mother moved north for work, and Winfrey lived with her grandmother in abject poverty. Some of her dresses were made from potato sacks. At six she went to live in Milwaukee with her mother; but at thirteen, after years of sexual abuse and rape by male relatives and friends of her mother, she fled. At fourteen she became pregnant. Her son died shortly after childbirth.[9]

Winfrey went to live in Tennessee with the man she believed to be her father. She flourished in high school and attracted attention for her skills in oratory and speech. She won a scholarship to Tennessee State University where she studied communication. She read news on a local radio station.

Television, however, allowed her to use all her formidable communication skills. By nineteen, she became the youngest anchor and the first African American woman television anchor in Nashville. She was destined for larger markets. She went to Baltimore to coanchor the news and, in a fateful move, to cohost a local talk show. Her affinity for this format was quickly obvious. Along with her communication skills, Winfrey brought empathy, wit, humor, and compassion to the show.

She was recruited for America's third-largest market and took over the low-rated *AM Chicago* talk show. The first show aired in January 1984. Within months, the show was at the top of the ratings. It was soon renamed *The Oprah Winfrey Show* and was extended to an hour. Broadcast nationally, it became the top-rated talk show in America. Winfrey used her success to remake the format and expand her topics. She explored health, politics, religion, and some of the most sensitive social issues of the time, such as child abuse and racism.

Still her success mounted. She became a movie star with a role in *The Color Purple*, for which she received an Oscar nomination. She cofounded Oxygen, a women's cable television channel. She founded Harpo (*Oprah* spelled backward), a multimedia production company that has launched television shows such as *Dr. Phil* and *Rachael Ray*, and *O, the Oprah Magazine*, not to mention feature films and radio shows. In 2011, Harpo established its own cable network, OWN, the Oprah Winfrey Network. She has established numerous philanthropic projects, including the Oprah Winfrey Leadership Academy for Girls in South Africa.

Winfrey is now sometimes called the most powerful woman in the world.[10] She is a self-made billionaire.[11] She is watched by millions around the globe in 140 countries. Of particular interest, she has become one of the most popular and admired figures—a role model and hero—among women throughout the world. For example, her show consistently ranks among the highest rated in the Middle East. One Arab satellite channel simply showed continual reruns of the program.[12] Winfrey's triumph over adversity resonates among women in oppressed countries and offers an exemplar of feminine freedom and power in male-dominated societies. Yale University noted this influence with a conference titled "Global Oprah: Celebrity as Transnational Icon."[13]

NO GLOBALIZATION WITHOUT MEDIA

Why even study globalization? It's a vague, opaque, difficult, and frankly ugly word. However, no matter how you feel about the word, globalization has shaped your world. And globalization *will* shape your world. From the food you eat, to the cell phone you use, to the schools you attend, to the air you breathe, globalization has its influence. Too, no field of work or study has been untouched by globalization. If you understand how globalization is shaping your field, you will have an advantage over others. Globalization is worth your attention.

Many books study globalization by pairing it with another concept, such as globalization and identity, globalization and human rights, globalization and culture, or globalization and terrorism. Such studies are extremely important. But I think the pairing of globalization and media offers something different. This book hopes to give special insights into globalization, not only by looking at the impact of globalization on media, but also at the impact of media on globalization.

In fact, this book will suggest that the media are the "significant other" of globalization. I will argue that globalization could not occur without media, that globalization and media act in concert and cohort, and that the two have partnered throughout the whole of human history. The opening vignettes are designed to emphasize the role of media in global events. From cave paintings to papyrus to printing presses to television to Facebook, media have made globalization possible.

I do not think I am indulging in hyperbole here, or building up my field of journalism and communication. And I certainly do not believe that the media have always been positive and progressive in their influence. But I look at the span of globalization across time, in economics, politics, and culture, and see media as essential in every phase. Could global trade have evolved without a flow of information on markets, prices, commodities, and more? Could empires have stretched across the world without communication throughout them? Could religion, music, poetry, film, fiction, cuisine, and fashion have developed as they have without the intermingling of media and culture? Globalization and media have proceeded together through time.

With such a claim, I am entering a sometimes virulent debate over the role of technology in society. The debate may seem like an ivory tower concern, but the issues are real. What *was* the role of Facebook and other social media in the 2011 Egyptian revolution? What was the role of the printing press in the Protestant Reformation? What is the role of television in the emancipation of women in Saudi Arabia? Technological determinists argue that technology shapes human events. Social determinists argue that humans shape technology in their pursuit of pleasure, power, and profit. These are some of the intriguing issues and questions that a focus on globalization and media can raise.

GLOBALIZATION AND MEDIA AS HUMAN ACTIONS

But wait. Can we really talk about globalization and media as "they"? Can we track "them" through history? Can we do something about "them"? One important theme of this book is that globalization and media are *not* abstract, unknowable, inevitable, inexorable forces of economics and technology. They are not out of the control of human hands. They have been and will be created by *people*. They are the result of human actions, or what academics call "human agency." It is hard to understand "globalization" and "media." It is not hard to understand the actions of Egyptian Facebook activists or Martin Luther or Oprah Winfrey or the head of the World Bank or Walt Disney or the CEO of News Corporation.

Because I am a professor, I will later give dry, dense, detailed definitions for *globalization* and *media*. But for now, a perfectly good definition of *globalization* is anytime anyone does anything anywhere across borders. And a perfectly good definition of *media* is anything people use to communicate. Those definitions work because they emphasize people and human action.

And so we will study the people whose actions have propelled what we now call globalization—immigrants, refugees, and tourists; missionaries, evangelists, and preachers; soldiers, conquerors, and diplomats; merchants, traders, and executives; scribes, poets, musicians, and writers. And we will study those who have employed what we now call media—cave painters, village messengers, town criers, and early printers; chief executive officers, chief financial officers, and advertising executives; movie studio executives, filmmakers, and actors; broadcast heads, television anchors, and camera operators; editors, reporters, and photographers; radio disk jockeys, bloggers, and cell phone users. Through these people, we will see that the media have been central to globalization. And we will understand how globalization and media together have helped create our world today and perhaps how they can create a better world tomorrow.

KEVIN CARTER: PULITZER PRIZE, THEN SUICIDE

The photograph was compelling and disturbing. A half-naked, emaciated African child has collapsed in the dust while crawling to get to a United Nations food camp. Her head is bowed to the dirt as if she is in prayer. Behind the child is perched a plump vulture. It is stalking the child. It is waiting for her to die.

The photograph was taken during a famine in the Sudan. Kevin Carter, the independent photographer who also stalked the child and shot the scene, would later say he waited about twenty minutes, hoping the vulture would spread its wings for a better photograph. It never did. Carter thus took his photograph, chased the bird away, and watched the little girl lift her head and continue her crawl forward. He never found out what happened to her. Afterward, he said, he sat under a tree, lit a cigarette, and cried.[14]

The *New York Times* bought and published the photo. It was an immediate sensation and was reprinted in newspapers and magazines around the world. Carter was awarded his profession's highest honor, the Pulitzer Prize for photography. Two months after receiving the Pulitzer, Carter attached a green garden hose to his red pickup truck in South Africa, turned on the truck, ran the hose into his house, and killed himself with carbon monoxide poisoning. He was thirty-three.[15]

PREMATURE CELEBRATIONS OF GLOBALIZATION

This book emphasizes the role of media in globalization. Yet it does not celebrate that role. Many books do celebrate globalization. They proclaim that the world is flat. They suggest that globalization has opened possibilities for all. They extol "the rise of the rest" in a post-American world. They especially credit communication technology and the media with making the world smaller and bringing together a global community. They look to globalization and the media to break down barriers between nations, increase opportunity, enhance cultural understanding, and create new cultural forms for representing and celebrating this globalized world.

I think the celebrations are premature. Globalization and media have indeed enriched the lives of many. But I want the story of Kevin Carter, which I tell in my classes, to sober us and remind us of the despair that still grips much of the world. The photograph was actually taken long ago, in 1993. Yet despite globalization, despite all our progress, scenes just like it still happen in Africa every day. Yes, globalization offers opportunity. Billions of people have improved their lot. But a billion more people, like that little girl, have been left behind. One billion people still suffer from extreme hunger; twenty-five thousand people, mostly children, die *every day* from starvation. Every day. Statistics don't capture the horror. Starvation is a cruel, terrible death. It is a withering of the body that takes place over months and months until death. The little girl whom Kevin Carter photographed was withering away. It still happens twenty-five thousand times a day in our world. We cannot yet celebrate globalization.

The starvation of children does not happen simply because of poverty and famine. Other human forces, too, roil our world, forces shaped by globalization and media. Neighbors slaughter neighbors in ethnic conflicts. Religious leaders plant discord that pits believers against one another. Corrupt rulers foment internecine warfare while enriching their own coffers. Pirates, drug lords, and militias still prowl villages and seas. Companies rape the environment and rob the land of its ability to nurture and support. Obscenely rich classes lead extravagant, wasteful lives while others wither in their shadows. We will see how human actors have shaped globalization and media to construct such a world. We cannot yet celebrate.

Many in the media, like Kevin Carter, strive to capture the tragedies of our world and to hear the cry of the poor and afflicted. They risk their lives to better the world. But too often the media are instead complacent, satisfied with pictures over understanding, conflict over content, profit over purpose. The media amuse and distract rather than disturb and focus. The media excel at entertainment and escape. They too often allow us to avoid the real troubles of the world with barking broadcasters, lavish films, soothing songs, endless e-mail, and infinite networking. At times, the media are even complicit in the division and deprivation that disfigure this globe. They profit from tragedy. They produce a "pornography of grief." No one can know exactly what tortured the soul of Kevin Carter. But he saw much of the anguish and misery of our world. He despaired over his own role. He left a suicide note. He said, "I'm really, really sorry. The pain of life overrides the joy to the point that joy does not exist." And so we cannot celebrate.

However, we can work to bring closer a time of celebration. Thus, this is not a book that disparages globalization. This is not a book that degrades the media. I believe that globalization and media are inherent to human experience. I believe that powerful actors have shaped globalization and media for their own purposes but that other actors can work to understand, direct, and improve globalization and media. We can first ask that globalization and media do their part to ease the suffering in the world, suffering that they themselves have helped to create. We can then look forward to a time when the benefits spawned by globalization and media truly are global.

MARSHALL MCLUHAN AND THE GLOBAL VILLAGE

The study of globalization and media might seem contemporary and new. But one of the earliest champions of globalization and media was the Canadian media scholar Marshall McLuhan, whose work began in the

1950s. We will look closely at his work in a later chapter. I want to introduce him now because he provides a concept in my book's subtitle. In one of his important formulations, McLuhan said that the media were making the world "smaller" and bringing people closer together. He famously predicted that the media would transform the world into a "global village."[16]

The metaphor captured the imagination of many people, and even today you can find thousands of references to the "global village." The phrase seems to creatively conjure the best hopes for globalization. It suggests that globalization and media have brought our divided world closer together. It suggests community and fellowship. It suggests, in McLuhan's words, "universal understanding and unity."[17]

I use the metaphor of the global village in my subtitle because this book will argue that McLuhan got it right—and terribly wrong. Slowly, fitfully, McLuhan's vision of a global village is being fulfilled. However, our village seems far from universal understanding and unity. Instead, these partners, globalization and media, I will show, are combining to create a dark and divided village, a village of gated communities and border walls, vigilantes and refugees, hunters and hunted, garrisons and ghettos, suffering and surfeit, beauty and decay, alienation and mediation.[18] Indeed, a focus on globalization and media today yields a clearer if bleaker vision of an emerging world, a darker but richer perspective, a global village of Babel.

BABEL

I want to explain here the final metaphor of my subtitle. The biblical story of Babel is found in the Book of Genesis, 11:1–9. In this story, humanity is united, and all people speak a common language: "The whole earth was of one language, and of one speech." Humans feel quite good about themselves. They feel omnipotent and celebratory. They give in to their hubris and vanity. The people select a site and decide to build a tower to themselves, a monument to humanity, "whose top may reach unto heaven," where the Lord resides.

The Lord sees what they are doing, however. He is not pleased. He recognizes the challenge. He is angered at the conceit. He decides to "confound their language, that they may not understand one another's speech," and to scatter them abroad. And being the Lord, he can do that. In one stroke, the people no longer understand one another. They are frightened, confused, and suspicious. The site suddenly becomes a maelstrom of misunderstanding, division, and confusion. "Therefore is the name of it called

Babel; because the Lord did there confound the language of all the earth; and from thence did the Lord scatter them abroad upon the face of all the earth."

A powerful metaphor, this Judeo-Christian trope has entered common language. The dictionary defines *Babel* as a scene of noise and confusion, a place of division and turmoil. (A modern film, *Babel*, starring Brad Pitt and Cate Blanchett, used the term to highlight its portrayal of disorder and chaos. Yahoo! Babel Fish is a cleverly named text and Web page translation service.)[19]

McLuhan surveyed the dawn of electronic communication and felt that humanity was regaining what it had lost at Babel. Global media, he suggested, allow people to once again think and speak as one, to overcome their diverse languages. Millions, perhaps billions, of people, for example, view the same advertising images, news photos, television shows, and films. McLuhan also predicted the ability of computers to instantaneously translate languages (he would have appreciated Google Translate). Global media also allow people to overcome being scattered abroad "upon the face of all the earth" by in effect shrinking the earth and bringing people together no matter how far apart. Cell phones, webcams, and more allow people to communicate with and see each other as if they lived in—a global village. For McLuhan, then, the global village would overcome the division of language and bring about the restoration of unity known before Babel.

GLOBAL VILLAGE OF BABEL

This book thus brings together two exceedingly potent metaphors. Globalization and media have indeed created the conditions by which the world can be conceived as a global village. Yet, contrary to what McLuhan first believed, globalization and media have helped construct a village degraded once again by humankind's hubris, vanity, and greed. It is a village characterized not by understanding and unity, but a village torn by avarice, strife, and suffering. Rather than overcoming Babel, humans have re-created a global village of Babel.

Humankind has been confounded once again by "power and greed and corruptible seed," as Bob Dylan sang. The modern world of globalization is marked by stark inequality, not only among nations but within nations. Seeds of division can be found everywhere, in our neighborhoods and in our continents. Experts warn of even darker days ahead. Leslie Gelb could not be more pessimistic. He draws from vast experience. A Pulitzer

Prize winner, former correspondent for the *New York Times*, senior official in State and Defense departments, president emeritus and senior fellow of the Council on Foreign Relations, Gelb foresees a world torn from within:

> a steady stream of internal conflicts and genocidal bloodlettings, a cascade of failed and failing states, whiffs of renewed nasty competition among great powers, a wildfire of international crime, and worries about worldwide health pandemics, food shortages, environmental disasters, rampant religious extremism, threatening economic depression, and a ceaseless, deadly international terrorist threat.[20]

Yikes! Babel seems tame in comparison. Can we forestall or avoid those days? I'm reminded of the scene in Charles Dickens' *A Christmas Carol*. Scrooge has just been given a terrifying glimpse of the future by the Ghost of Christmas Yet to Come, and he beseechingly asks the Ghost, "Are these the shadows of the things that Will be, or are they shadows of the things that May be, only?" We will not have a chance to alter the shadows of the things that may be unless we at least understand how we arrived at this time and place. This book is an exploration of how our global village of Babel has come to be created through the interaction of two essential and entwined forces: globalization and media.

Our steps will unfold progressively. We will first look at what we mean when we talk about *globalization* and *media*. Much of the confusion around these terms stems from differences in language and meaning. We will want to be clear what we mean by them. With our terms straight, we will then go back in history. We will trace the development of media from humanity's first days and show how globalization and media have proceeded together through time in the construction of this modern world.

Then we will be ready to look at our world. We will study the work of scholars and theorists who point out a most important fact of our time: globalization and media have created the conditions through which many people can now *imagine* themselves as part of one world. It is this *global imaginary* that brings to fruition McLuhan's global village. We will then look at life in the emerging global village. We will break down the vague abstraction of "globalization" into the three most important domains in which people have acted globally: economics, politics, and culture. It is mostly within these three realms that globalization plays out in each epoch, every day; and we will see that the media are vital to all three.

Our focus will remain on people—humans making decisions and taking actions that have consequences for other humans. Some people, we will learn, strive heroically to bring about a world of justice and community.

Others use their powers to enrich themselves and degrade and impoverish others. We will confirm that the global village is right now a place of division and woe, not unity and peace. We will recognize that globalization and media have failed to keep their promise to humankind and instead have combined to produce the vast wealth and woe that mark our world. And we will suggest ways forward for a better world.

KEN BANKS: POVERTY? THERE'S AN APP FOR THAT

I have spent most of my life working, teaching, and researching in journalism and media. I have spent much time traveling the globe. I believe that globalization and the media together do have the power to transform this "weary world of woe." I want to join the celebration of globalization and media. I cannot yet. But I am a hopeful person, and I remain hopeful.

Here is one reason for hope: Ken Banks was a successful staffer for global information and technology companies in England. His skills with software development had taken him to various corporate and media positions. He helped introduce digital television in parts of England. He understood and profited from the forces of globalization and media. Then Ken Banks did something extraordinary. He stepped back from the corporate world and put his considerable talents to work at a seemingly insurmountable task—using information technology to improve the lives of billions in Africa.[21]

In 2003, he created kiwanja.net, an organization that devotes itself to the application of mobile technology for social and environmental change in the developing world, particularly in Africa. Banks adopted the name, he says, because he was determined to avoid names that evoked technology. He wanted instead a name that evokes how people interact with technology. In Kiswahili, *kiwanja* can have numerous definitions, but Banks was attracted to its meaning as "a place to meet."[22]

In particular, he wanted to develop technology that could provide a place to meet for grassroots nonprofit organizations and the people they hoped to serve, in health, economics, education, poverty, and more. The challenges were formidable. Much of sub-Saharan Africa suffers from desperate circumstances. There is little communication infrastructure, such as telephone lines, radio towers, television cables, and Internet access. Relatively few people have landline telephones, radios, televisions, or computers. But Banks knew that many people have cell phones. In fact, Africans have a billion of them, and cell phone use is growing faster in Africa than anywhere else in the world. People don't need electricity or cables or wires or expensive equipment or computer skills to use a cell phone. Close to 80 percent of the people in Africa have a phone, and almost everyone has access to a cell phone.

Most of the cell phones in Africa are basic phones, not smart phones with Web access and multimedia capabilities. (The most popular phone in Africa by far is the humble Nokia 1100, created in 2003.) But the phones can all receive text messages. This is the beauty of Ken Banks' software, such as Frontline SMS and nGOmobile. It allows any nonprofit group to communicate text messages that can instantaneously reach hundreds, even thousands, of people in two-way communication. A health care group can send a message about the availability of a vaccine or a reminder to take medication. A farmers' collective can share information about crop diseases or an advance in fertilizer. Fishermen can send news of a change in market prices. A civic group can foster citizen engagement by monitoring national elections and reporting on the activities of government officials. An education group can send a text with instructional material or news about the availability of classes. In more than fifty countries, across Africa and around the world, Ken Banks' software is improving the lives of thousands, perhaps millions. That is reason for hope.

LU GUANG: DOCUMENTING THE HUMAN CONDITION

Here is another reason for hope—another photographer, a chapter bookend perhaps for Kevin Carter. Lu Guang was twenty-one, a Chinese factory worker in Zhejiang Province. He had a hobby: he had been taking photographs since his teens. In 1993, he took a risk, quit his job, and enrolled at a fine arts academy in Beijing. His talent was evident to all, and he graduated with honors. Forsaking the financial allure of fine art or commercial photography after graduation, Lu Guang took another risk. He decided instead to use his talents to capture some of the social and economic troubles facing his country.

His photographs chronicle the ravaging effects of globalization on the Chinese people. One project records the misery of poor peasants in Henan Province who sold their blood and ended up infected with HIV. The scarred and withered bodies portray not only the ravages of AIDS but the desperation that drives people to sell their very blood. Another project depicts the social and environmental devastation that has accompanied China's industrial revolution. Other ventures include photographic essays on the SARS epidemic, drug addiction at the Burmese border, and industrial and chemical pollution.

Lu has now begun to receive international acclaim for his work. He was the first photographer from China to be invited by the U.S. Department of State as a visiting scholar. He won the Henri Nannan Prize for Photography in Germany and a grant from *National Geographic*. He also received the W. Eugene Smith Grant in Humanistic Photography, an award to photographers "who have demonstrated a deep commitment to documenting the human condition."[23] Lu Guang and others strive to document the human condition in our global village. They give us another reason for hope in globalization and media.

2

LANGUAGE AND METAPHOR

What We Talk about When We Talk about Globalization and Media

THE BATTLE OF SEATTLE

On November 30, 1999, ministers and officials of the World Trade Organization (WTO) were set to meet at the Washington State Convention and Trade Center in Seattle, Washington. These men and women, some of the most powerful economic policy makers on the planet, meet annually to discuss regulations on global trade and other financial issues. But that morning, few delegates made it from their hotels to the convention center.

They were astonished to find more than forty thousand angry demonstrators clogging the streets around the convention center. Protesters chained themselves together in key intersections, allowing no vehicles to pass. Others lay down in the street. Chaos and violence erupted. Protesters fought with riot police. Marchers were turned back by tear gas, batons, and rubber bullets. Store windows were smashed and dumpsters set ablaze. The bedlam continued over the next three days. It was one of the biggest demonstrations in the United States since the Vietnam War. It came to be known as the Battle of Seattle.[1]

The focus of the protest: globalization.

Most people have trouble defining *globalization*. The word seems to mean so many things—a global economy, growing prosperity in China and India, international travel and communication, immigration, migration, more foreign films and foods, McDonald's in Paris, Starbucks in Africa, mosques in New York, an increase in "global" problems such as climate change and terrorism. The word, as I mention in the preface, means everything and nothing.

Yet Seattle drew forty thousand people (some say close to one hundred thousand people) from around the world to protest this thing called globalization. Who were they? American labor unions who felt that their jobs were being given to low-wage workers in other countries. Farmers from poor nations who felt that U.S. trade policies unfairly protected U.S. farmers. Environmentalists who felt that clean air and water were being sacrificed so industries could profit. Religious groups who felt that child labor was being allowed and encouraged in some countries. Social justice groups who felt that world economic policies privileged the powerful and took advantage of the weak.

The demonstrations were quickly labeled "antiglobalization" in the West. Mainstream media were swift to condemn. Thomas Friedman's column the very next day in the *New York Times* was titled "Senseless in Seattle." It began,

> Is there anything more ridiculous in the news today than the protests against the World Trade Organization in Seattle? I doubt it. These anti-W.T.O. protesters—who are a Noah's ark of flat-earth advocates, protectionist trade unions and yuppies looking for their 1960's fix—are protesting against the wrong target with the wrong tools.[2]

But others gave credence to the protests. The *South China Morning Post* said, "The anti-liberalisation lobby has been sneeringly dismissed by some media critics as an undisciplined, irrational chorus against an unequivocal and irreversible trend. But despite the immovable self-belief of the high priests of globalisation, one must ask whether their opponents' grievances—however fractious, self interested and wide ranging—have some validity."[3]

And the protesters themselves denied that they were against globalization. Indeed, they said, the protests were a stunning example of global cooperation and action. Groups from around the world had organized and planned the demonstrations for months. The groups tried to make it clear that they were against exploitive economic and corporate globalization. And they used globalization against it.

How on earth does one make sense of this thing called globalization?

GLOBALIZATION, LANGUAGE, AND RAYMOND CARVER

The subtitle of this chapter is taken from a Raymond Carver short story, "What We Talk about When We Talk about Love." In the story, two married couples discuss their four very different, and ultimately starkly opposing, views of "real love." Any book about globalization must confront early the different and starkly opposing views of the word *globalization*. First used perhaps fifty years ago, and little used until thirty years ago, *globalization* has entered languages around the world. Yet people are still unsure what it means, when it began, or if it even exists. This difficulty does not offer an excuse, an easy way out. Globalization is affecting our lives in numerous ways. We should know about it. The word cannot be dismissed.

Like love, globalization is real. It exists. But its meaning will be different for every individual. How does one study that? Two ways. One, you study the concrete, *objective* processes that make up globalization—changes in economics, politics, and culture over time. We will do that in the chapters to come. But you also study the *subjective* processes—the language, metaphors, and meanings attached to globalization. The important thing here—the object of study—is what people *say* about love and *say* about globalization. Scholars would suggest that meaning arises "in discourse," in language. We need to know what we mean when we talk about globalization. The word will not go away. Though it is vast and vague, the word may portend nothing less than the future.

Anthony Giddens was among the first scholars to begin serious inquiry into globalization decades ago. In an interview, he marveled at the rapid acceptance of the term since the 1980s.

> At that time globalization was not a word used everywhere, as it is now. We have even started to feel a certain distaste for it. There cannot be many concepts in the social sciences that have been able to penetrate public consciousness the way globalization has. Globalization has already gone around the world. People have started talking about it, not just in academic discourse, but in general conversation. This is quite an extraordinary change in less than 20 years.[4]

This chapter focuses on the discourse, the conversation, the language of globalization. The economic, political, and cultural processes that make up globalization—the objective processes—will be discussed later. The focus now is on the language of—and about—globalization. Manfred Steger has stated it eloquently. He says, "Globalization is not merely an objective process but also a plethora of stories and metaphors—told, retold, and performed countless times—that define, describe, and analyze that very process."[5]

I will begin by discussing the origins and meanings of the contested term *globalization*. Its etymology yields surprising insights. I turn next to when globalization began. Even here, there is wild disagreement. Some scholars say thirty years ago. Some say one hundred thousand years ago. I will then look at how scholars, politicians, and institutions have talked about globalization, focusing specifically on metaphors for globalization. People often unknowingly use metaphors when talking about it. Globalization is understood as an era, an unstoppable force, a rising tide, a benefactor, a network, or another form of empire. It is wise to pay close attention to the metaphors that people and institutions employ when discussing globalization. These metaphors reveal much about the stance and understanding of those who use them. Finally, because the word can mean different things to different people, this book will offer its own definition of *globalization*, a definition that unsurprisingly emphasizes the role of media in globalization.

Media will be the focus of the next chapter. The word, of course, is plural for *medium*—a means of conveying something, such as a channel of communication. The plural form—*media*—only came into general circulation in the 1920s. Like *globalization*, the word *media* came into popular usage because a word was needed to talk about a new social issue. In the 1920s, people were talking about their fears over the harmful influence of these new "mass media," such as comic books, radio, and film. However, in the next chapter I will make the case that humans have used media of communication from their first days on earth, and that those media have been essential to globalization. And by the end of that chapter, we will be clear what we talk about when we talk about globalization and media.

-IZATION AND ITS DISCONTENTS

As a former journalist, and now a professor and writer, I have always cared about words. I don't care for the word *globalization*. *Globalization*, it must be acknowledged, is a distasteful word. *Global* rolls and lowers the tongue, as if one is getting ready to spit. *-Ization* buzzes through the teeth, machinelike and sterile. The combination—*globalization*—offers distance and frigidity. Overseas, in the Queen's English, the word gets softened to *globalisation*, but it is still chilly and distant. The French offer us *la mondialisation*. The Chinese say 全球化, *quan qiu hua*. In Kiswahili, it's *utandawazi*. No language, it seems, is comfortable with the word.

The word also has murky origins. Some say researchers have found references to it in the social sciences as early as the 1940s. Merriam-Webster's dictionary dates *globalize* to 1944. Theodore Levitt, a former professor at the Harvard Business School, is widely credited with popularizing the term, which he used in a 1983 *Harvard Business Review* article, "The Globalization of Markets." Despite its deficiencies and cloudy past, however, the word has exploded in prominence and usage.

I recently looked in the Library of Congress card catalog—the means by which the library recorded its vast holdings before 1980—and found one card that mentions globalization: *La Globalizacion de la Ensenanza* (The Globalization of Education), published in 1965 by a Mexican educator, Emilia Elias de Ballesteros. I then searched the library's online catalog, which records recent holdings, and got a message that said, "Your search retrieved more records than can be displayed. Only the first 10,000 will be shown." Nayan Chanda, former head of the Yale Center for the Study of Globalization, performed a similar exercise. He studied a database of eight thousand newspapers, magazines, and reports worldwide and found that in 1981 there were two references to globalization.[6] A Google search now brings up 15.1 million sites. Chanda nicely observes, "The term *globalization* emerged because the visibility of our globally connected life *called for a word* to sum up the phenomenon of this interconnectedness."[7]

Why did the world need this particular word? When I first started this book, Liah Greenfeld, an acclaimed scholar of nationalism, pointed out to me the implications of *-ation* words. They are nouns derived from verbs, she noted. "The importance of these *-ation* words," Greenfeld said, "is that they suggest the verb, the action, the process, is completed."[8] It is a good insight. The verb becomes a noun. Action has stopped. The process is completed. Creating has resulted in creation. Saturating has resulted in saturation. Capitulating has resulted in capitulation. *Globalization* exists uneasily, perhaps deceptively, in this family. Has globalizing resulted in globalization? Is the process really completed? *Globalization*, in this perspective, may claim too much.

Globalization, it turns out, has more etymological subtleties. The word resides in an even more specialized family: *-ization* words, nouns formed by a combination of *-ize* verbs and *-ation*. *-Ization*, my etymology dictionary tells me, is "a suffix that creates nouns indicating the process *or* outcome of doing something." Different from simple *-ation* words, *-ization* words are inconclusive. They can be process *or* outcome. If I speak of "the organization of the students," I might be speaking of the ongoing organizing of the students—I am trying to get them organized. Or I might be speaking of an already established student organization—the Student Senate is the organization of the students. Similarly, if I read of the modernization of the village, I do not know whether the village is in the process of being modernized or modernization has already been accomplished. *-Ization* words can have it both ways.

My focus on *-ization* is not my own idiosyncrasy. Other scholars, too, have considered the crucial ambiguity of *globalization* as an *-ization*.[9] Indeed, Peter J. Taylor finds the distinction between outcome and process essential for the study of globalization. He says, "There is an obvious first lesson to draw from this language trap: it is necessary to separate out the two meanings of the izations in any critical analysis."[10] He astutely points out, however, a second lesson: "Any critical analysis cannot dismiss an ization by exposing the weakness of just one of its two meanings."[11]

What does he mean? It is an especially important point in discussions of globalization. Writers too often will dismiss globalization and say it does not exist. They will suggest as evidence some global ideal, such as high percentages of global trade or global travel or global phone calls. They will find, unsurprisingly, lower percentages and conclude that by many measures, the world is not yet globalized. And they will be right. However, they will have proved only that globalization is not an accomplished *outcome*—but they will not have addressed the second meaning of the word—whether the world is undergoing the *process* of globalization. Taylor says, "Unsurprisingly, such a 'straw man' exercise can easily prove that we do not live in a global- ized world, but tells us little about the very real globalization tendencies we are experiencing."[12] When people argue about globalization, they may be arguing about two different things—a completed outcome or an ongoing process—an argument caused by -*ization*.

ANTIGLOBALIZATION? WORDS MATTER

I hope you see that my etymological focus is not weird, bookish indulgence. It may help explain some of the academic and political debates over global- ization. As an -*ization* word, *globalization* can be process *or* outcome. How someone understands and uses the word thus becomes critically important. Does a writer, politician, or economist believe that globalization is already an *outcome*—something accomplished, completed, and universal? Tony Blair, the former prime minister of Britain, believes so. "I hear people say we have to stop and debate globalization," he said in a speech. "You might as well debate whether autumn should follow summer."[13] Kofi Annan, the former secretary general of the United Nations, noted this dimension of the word: "It has been said that arguing against globalization is like arguing against the law of gravity."[14]

Or does someone believe that globalization is a *process* (or *processes*) that can be challenged, altered, or even reversed? Protesters who disrupt meet- ings of the World Trade Organization, the International Monetary Fund, and the World Bank think so. "Alter-globalization" advocates do too. They belong to a social movement that supports global interaction but opposes much economic globalization because they feel it disregards the environment, labor protection, indigenous cultures, and human rights.

Words matter greatly here. As we saw with the Battle of Seattle, people who protest economic globalization policies or try to alter other processes of globalization are often labeled "antiglobalization" by their opponents and the mass media. Many of the protesters detest and resist that term. They feel it masks and distorts their primary protest, which is focused against economic policies. And the label denies their long embrace of global cooperation and action. Linguist and political activist Noam Chomsky points out the battles being fought over such language:

> The term "globalization" has been appropriated by the powerful to refer to a specific form of international economic integration, one based on investor rights, with the interests of people incidental. That is why the business press, in its more honest moments, refers to the "free trade agreements" as "free investment agreements." Accordingly, advocates of other forms of globalization are described as "anti-globalization"; and some, unfortunately, even accept this term, though it is a term of propaganda that should be dismissed with ridicule. No sane person is opposed to globalization, that is, international integration. Surely not the left and the workers movements, which were founded on the principle of international solidarity—that is, globalization in a form that attends to the rights of people, not private power systems.[15]

Naomi Klein agrees. In *No Logo: Brands, Globalization and Resistance, The Shock Doctrine*, and other works, she challenges "the economic process that goes by the benign euphemism 'globalization' [which] now reaches into every aspect of life, transforming every activity and natural resource into a measured and owned commodity."[16] She points to links being made among landless farmers in Brazil, teachers in Argentina, fast-food workers in Italy, and migrant tomato pickers in Florida and says, "The irony of the media-imposed label, 'anti-globalization,' is that we in this movement have been turning globalization into a lived reality, perhaps more so than even the most multinational of corporate executives."[17] I look carefully when politicians or headlines label groups as "antiglobalization."

IMPERMANENCE AND CHANGE: *ANICCA*

This book is built on the premise that globalization is not an outcome but a process—indeed a host of processes, including economic, political, and cultural—that may be as old as humankind and that is ongoing today.

And it is important to stress that processes are not inevitable. They do not unfold inexorably. They stop and start and change course. Processes are also not independent. They conflict with, complement, or compromise other processes. Processes also are not progress. They can constrict and retard and bring penalty and pain. And processes may never reach an outcome or final state.

The Buddhist approach to globalization is especially process oriented and of great interest. In the Theravada Buddhist tradition, globalization is understood as a process of our globe. That is, globalization has been going on since our globe came into being, predating even humans. Globalization is an integral component of a larger dynamic, *anicca*, which is impermanence and change.[18] There is much to appreciate in that conception. Perhaps, as Theravada Buddhists proclaim, the processes of globalization will continue throughout time. That is something to think about: globalization will be occurring long after humans have left the globe.

WHEN DID GLOBALIZATION BEGIN?

People cannot agree on what globalization is. They also cannot agree on when it began. Some scholars feel that globalization is a decidedly modern phenomenon. It began a few decades ago, they say, in the late 1900s, when advances in media and transportation technology truly globalized the world. The cultural anthropologist Arjun Appadurai, a scholar I greatly admire, feels there was a "rupture" within social life in the late twentieth century. He says that advances in media, such as television, computers, and cell phones, combined with changes in migration patterns, such as people more easily flowing back and forth around the world. Those two "diacritics"—media and migration—fundamentally changed human life, Appadurai says, and gave rise to this thing now called globalization.[19]

However, many other scholars say globalization began a few hundred years ago. They pair globalization with the rise of modernity in the Enlightenment or with the age of European exploration. Columbus's arrival in America is often used as a marker for globalization. Some of these scholars are coyly provocative. The historian Robert Marks, for example, baldly states that globalization began in 1571 in Manila. His reason: Spain's colonization of the Philippines in that year was the final link in a truly global trade route.[20]

Still others feel that globalization has been going on since the beginning of humanity, when the first *Homo sapiens* departed from other *Homo sapiens* in an African village and set out in search of food or water or adventure. Those first travelers of the world put globalization into motion. Yale's Nayan Chanda embraces this view. He says globalization "is a process that has worked silently for millennia without having been given a name" and that, as a trend, globalization "has been with us since the beginning of history." He argues that a multitude of threads "connect us to faraway places from an ancient time."[21]

I have great affection for this view of globalization as a historical process as old as humankind. And I think plenty of evidence can be mustered to support this long-term view. I see economic globalization in the Silk Road, the storied trade routes that connected Asia with the Mediterranean world as early as 200 BCE. I see cultural globalization in the spread of Islam from Mecca in the seventh century to a billion people around the world today. I see political globalization in the ancient empires of Egypt, Mesopotamia, and Persia that spanned much of the known world, influencing culture, politics, and economics for centuries to come.

No right answer exists, of course, as to when globalization began. Writers—and readers—simply must make clear what they believe and why. Me? I embrace the concept that there is a fundamental human impulse toward globalization. I believe there is an innate desire in people to wonder, to wander, to explore, to set out, to seek a better life, or perhaps just to find a different life. I can agree with Appadurai that globalization has accelerated and intensified in our time. But globalization, for me, has been a part of humanity from its first steps.

METAPHORS OF GLOBALIZATION

Armed with this linguistic and historical knowledge of globalization, we can now enter ongoing debates. We know that academic, social, and political discussions of globalization are complicated because the word itself is complicated—a verb turned into a noun that can mean process or outcome. But there are further complications, because when people talk about globalization, they often employ metaphors that have large implications.

Studies of metaphor often begin with Aristotle, whose *Poetics* provides a simple and clarifying definition: "Metaphor consists in giving the thing a name that belongs to something else."[22] A metaphor thus is a figure of speech that brings together two unlike things. "The prime minister was *under fire* because of his vote." The prime minister, hopefully, was not really under fire. The sentence borrows war language as a metaphor to make its point. "The democracy was in its *infancy*." One word, *infancy*, can say a lot. The democracy, like an infant, is in its very early stages of development. Too, the democracy, like an infant, might be vulnerable and in need of aid and support.

Metaphor is different from simile, which draws a simple comparison. "The prime minister is *as stubborn as a mule*." All the words in this sentence keep their original meaning. We are learning something about the prime minister, but we are not reconceiving him as something different. "The prime minister shot down any talk of reform." Here, we are back to metaphor, unless of course the prime minister really did start firing guns on reform. Through metaphor, humans compare something familiar to something unfamiliar so they can make better sense of the unfamiliar or portray something a certain way.

Building on Aristotle, study of metaphor has long been undertaken in rhetoric, speech, literature, linguistics, pragmatics, psychology, philosophy, cognitive science, and many other fields.[23] Scholars have come to believe that metaphors are much more than rhetorical flourishes employed by writers, poets, and playwrights. In *The Rule of Metaphor, Interpretation Theory*, and other works, philosopher Paul Ricoeur argues that metaphors are used by everyone and provide new ways of describing and understanding things. He finds that "a metaphor, in short, tells us something new about reality."[24]

Indeed, some cognitive psychologists now believe that metaphors are essential to human understanding, an inescapable aspect of human thought. Neither good nor bad, metaphor may be the only way for humans to comprehend profound and complex issues, such as life, death, sickness, health, war, and peace. We make sense of these things by comparing them to something else. *Metaphors We Live By* has become an important touchstone for social and political discussions of metaphor. In that volume, Lakoff and Johnson argue that the human conceptual system indeed is fundamentally metaphoric, that metaphors structure the way people think, and that humans think of things as something else. Lakoff and Johnson find that metaphors "are not just a matter of language, but of thought and reason."[25]

So what are some common metaphors for globalization? You won't be surprised to learn that researchers have looked carefully at the language used to discuss globalization. For example, in *Metaphors of Globalization*, Kornprobst, Pouliot, Shah, and Zaiotti gather together a dozen essays on the topic. Their subtitle provides a sense of the variety: *Mirrors, Magicians and Mutinies*.[26] In my own research, I have tracked key metaphors of globalization used by world leaders and the media. I have found six that often get used—and abused. I'm sure there are many other metaphors for globalization, but surely you will see these six often.

Globalization as Our Era

Let's go back to the quote on globalization by Tony Blair, the former prime minister of Britain. He said, "I hear people say we have to stop and debate globalization. You might as well debate whether autumn should follow summer." He went on, "In the era of rapid globalization, there is no mystery about what works—an open, liberal economy, prepared constantly to change to remain competitive."[27] What does that quote reveal about Blair's thought and reason? For Blair, globalization is a time, like the coming of the seasons, the "era" of globalization. The metaphor is a temporal one. The time for globalization has arrived. We are in an era of globalization. It is of our time. Many people employ this metaphor. For example, Chinese ambassador Zhang Yesui titled a policy speech "China and China-US Relations in the Era of Globalization."[28]

The words seem natural, which is why the metaphor is so powerful. But hidden in the metaphor are a host of assumptions: Globalization is modern, of this era, not previous eras. Globalization is indeed an outcome, not a process, and that outcome has been achieved in our time. Globalization is an accomplished fact. One cannot turn back the hands of time. When Representative Sander M. Levin, a Democrat from Michigan and an expert on trade policy, took over the powerful post of chairman of the U.S. House Ways and Means Committee, he proclaimed, "I know globalization is here to stay."[29] Many, many books have been produced using the metaphor of globalization as our era: *Territoriality and Conflict in an Era of Globalization, Islam in an Era of Globalization, Industrial Policy in an Era of Globalization.* I was tempted to title this section "Globalization in an Era of Globalization."

Globalization as Unstoppable Force

You may have noticed that Kofi Annan, the former secretary general of the United Nations, used a different metaphor in an earlier paragraph. He said, "It has been said that arguing against globalization is like arguing against the law of gravity."[30] The metaphor is not a temporal one. It depicts globalization as an unstoppable force of nature. Annan was actually arguing against this metaphor but had to acknowledge its power. Who can argue against gravity? The metaphor of globalization as unstoppable force is often used. When people or institutions talk about globalization as inevitable, inexorable, or irresistible, they are relying upon this metaphor.

In *The Lexus and the Olive Tree*, Thomas Friedman places globalization within this metaphor. He says, "Globalization involves *the inexorable integration* of markets, nation-states and technologies to a degree never witnessed before—in a way that is enabling individuals, corporations and nation-states to reach around the world farther, faster, deeper and cheaper than ever before."[31] The *New York Times* recognized the metaphor and placed a fun headline over a review of Friedman's book: "The Global Village Is Here. Resist at Your Peril."[32]

The Roman Catholic Church has also portrayed globalization in terms of an inexorable force—which has led to new sins. The Vatican's official newspaper, *L'Osservatore Romano*, published an interview with Gianfranco Girotti, head of the Apostolic Penitentiary. Girotti announced an updated list of mortal sins. The newcomers were social sins, such as pollution, genetic engineering, and social injustice, which were to be added to the original seven deadly sins of pride, envy, gluttony, greed, lust, wrath, and sloth. The reason for adding the new sins, according to the church representative, was the inexorable force of globalization. Girotti said, "New sins have appeared on the horizon of humanity as a corollary of the *unstoppable process* of globalization."[33]

Similarly, the CEO of Credit Suisse Group, Oswald J. Grübel, calls globalization "unstoppable." He states, "It's a fact that globalization is in full swing and there really is no stopping it anymore. . . . So it's really quite pointless to talk in terms of yes or no to globalization."[34] Author Gregg Easterbrook writes that globalization is proceeding at "Mach speed." He compares globalization to a sonic boom. "What is occurring now is a Sonic Boom—noisy, superfast, covering huge amounts of territory."[35] Resist at your peril.

Globalization as a Rising Tide

Nature provides another powerful metaphor for globalization: the tide, or, often, the rising tide. In this metaphor, globalization is a development as natural as the incoming tide on an ocean beach. The metaphor also has a temporal quality because the tide rises at a certain time—our time. U.S. president Barack Obama has used this metaphor. Speaking in Flint, Michigan, during the 2008 campaign, Obama offered a vision of a new world, "a picture of a world where old boundaries are disappearing; a world where communication, connection, and competition can come from anywhere." And, he said,

There are some who believe that we must try to turn back the clock on this new world; that the only chance to maintain our living standards is to build a fortress around America; to stop trading with other countries, shut down immigration, and rely on old industries. I disagree. Not only is it impossible to turn back the tide of globalization, but efforts to do so can make us worse off.[36]

Similarly, in a speech to the Chinese Economic Association annual conference, Ambassador Zha Peixin said, "In this massive tide of economic globalisation, no country can develop and prosper in isolation. China has learnt from her long history that isolation leads to backwardness." He went on to describe the tide in even stronger terms: "How to turn disadvantages into advantages in the tidal wave of globalisation depends on formulating the correct policies and strategies."[37] The tide has become a tidal wave.

Others often add to this tidal metaphor. They say globalization is a "rising tide that will lift all boats." The metaphor suggests that globalization will elevate and enrich all, not just a few. The implications of that metaphor have been recognized and specifically resisted by the UN's Kofi Annan as well as his successor, Ban Ki-moon. In his farewell address to the UN General Assembly, Annan said, "My friends, globalization is not a tide that lifts all boats. Even among those who are benefiting, many are deeply insecure and strongly resent the apparent complacency of those more fortunate than themselves. So globalization, which in theory brings us all closer together, in practice risks driving us further apart."[38] Three years later, speaking to the World Economic Forum in Davos, Switzerland, Ban Ki-moon took up the same theme. Looking back over the previous years, he said, "Yes, globalization had lifted many from poverty. Yet the spread of free markets and capital did not raise all boats. In fact, it hurt many of the world's poorest people."[39]

The International Forum on Globalization, a research and educational group, neatly turns back the tidal metaphor. It says, "While promoters of globalization proclaim that this model is the rising tide that will lift all boats, citizen movements find that it is instead lifting only yachts."[40]

Globalization as Benefactor

I was tempted to title this metaphor "Globalization as Santa Claus." This metaphor humanizes and personifies globalization as a munificent figure who distributes benefits. Proponents of economic globalization often refer to the many benefits it brings. They argue that globalization "lifts" people out of poverty. Writing in *Forbes*, Robyn Meredith and Suzanne Hoppough argue "Why Globalization Is Good." They say,

The protesters and do-gooders are just plain wrong. It turns out global-ization is good—and not just for the rich, but especially for the poor. The booming economies of India and China—the Elephant and the Dragon—have lifted 200 million people out of abject poverty in the 1990s as globalization took off, the International Monetary Fund says. Tens of millions more have catapulted themselves far ahead into the middle class.[41]

Globalization is almost heroic. It brings good. It lifts people up. When then-President George W. Bush spoke to the World Bank, he too painted the benefits of globalization in glowing terms. "Vast regions and nations from Chile to Thailand are escaping the bonds of poverty and oppression by embracing markets and trade and new technologies," he said. "What some call globalization is in fact the triumph of human liberty stretching across national borders. And it holds the promise of delivering billions of the world's citizens from disease and hunger and want."[42]

Globalization as Networked World

Communication technology provides the backdrop for this meta-phor, which emphasizes the global connections allowed by advances in communication and transportation. In this metaphor, borders and bar-riers between people have come down as world networks draw people increasingly together. *The Rise of the Network Society*, by Manuel Castells, is an in-depth scholarly exploration of the implications of a networked world.[43]

The metaphor also appears in numerous popular formulations. Thomas Friedman's *The World Is Flat* and Kenichi Ohmae's *The Borderless World* are based on the metaphor of a world networked and connected by globalization and media. For example, in a borderless world, Ohmae con-cludes, "globalization mandates alliances, makes them absolutely essential to strategy."[44] Friedman writes with his typical enthusiasm that "the most exciting part" of globalization and the flattening of the world is "the fact that we are now in the process of connecting all the knowledge pools in the world together," and "by connecting all these knowledge pools we are on the cusp of an incredible new era of innovation, an era that will be driven from left field and right field, from West and East and from North and South."[45]

You will note that my own metaphor of the global village of Babel borrows too from the idea of globalization as a world made smaller and more connected by communication. Similarly, in a speech to the United

Nations, Tariq Khaddam Alfayez of Saudi Arabia brought together the global village with the metaphor of the networked world. He said,

> Globalization means lifting off geographic, cultural and social barriers; and the mingling of human cultures and civilizations with one another through the revolution of technology, communication and information that intensified the speed and volume of communications, interactions, and human and economic activities. In the light of globalization, the human community becomes one unit or one small village.[46]

Similarly, former Brazilian president Luiz Inacio Lula da Silva saw countries networked through globalization. He said, "One country relies on the other. And everybody knows that if we detach ourselves from the right decision, it would cause loss, damage. And I trust the maturity of the leaders, the political leaders, and I believe the globalization allows that we would have to build more and more common policies among us."[47] Lula used the metaphor of a networked world to make his case for common action.

Globalization as Empire

Is globalization just another name for age-old empire building? This metaphor most often aligns globalization with the economic and military expansion of a Western, or American, empire. The metaphor of globalization as empire is most often used to raise passion and protest. Poor people and poor countries are urged to resist being overtaken by globalization as empire. Hardt and Negri, for example, equate globalization with traditional notions of empire. Like empire, they say, globalization is expanding economically and politically, overcoming borders or boundaries. They note that over the past decades, "we have witnessed an irresistible and irreversible globalization of economic and cultural exchanges." They go on to say, "Empire is the political subject that effectively regulates these global exchanges."[48] Hardt and Negri call for resistance to empire: "The passage to Empire and its processes of globalization offer new possibilities to the forces of liberation."[49]

Arundhati Roy, author of the novel *The God of Small Things*, has become a celebrated activist against "corporate globalization," which she also identifies as empire. In *An Ordinary Person's Guide to Empire*, Roy calls for opposition to corporate globalization, which she feels works in concert with American empire. Like Hardt and Negri, Roy uses the metaphor as a cause for hope in the battle against corporate globalization. She writes, "Suddenly the inevitability of the project of corporate globalization is beginning to seem more than a little evitable."[50]

"METAPHORS TO GLOBALIZE BY"

Each of the preceding metaphors reveals a way of thinking about globalization. Some of them are in stark contrast, even opposition. However, they are all useful for the study of globalization. If a politician speaks about the inexorable, unstoppable force of globalization, I have a pretty good sense of how she views globalization. If a scholar writes about the imperialist tendencies of empire and corporate globalization, I understand that view as well. Through metaphor, I can understand what they talk about when they talk about globalization.

In *Metaphors to Live By*, Lakoff and Johnson emphasize that metaphors organize and express experience. Metaphors can become ways of thinking about something, such as globalization. In the conclusion of *Metaphors of Globalization*, the editors nicely acknowledge Lakoff and Johnson with their chapter title "Metaphors to Globalize By." It is a fitting tribute. And the editors affirm that metaphors of globalization "cast experiences in terms of something else, a move that comes with huge political, social, cultural and economic effects."[51]

Because metaphors can organize and structure people's thinking, leaders, groups, and institutions often try to control metaphoric language. Metaphors sometimes battle for supremacy (metaphorically, of course). People against legalized abortion, for example, use the word *pro-life* rather than *antiabortion*. People in favor of legalized abortion use *pro-choice* rather than *proabortion*. Metaphors of globalization are also contested. Two successive United Nations secretary generals have specifically resisted the metaphor of "the rising tide" of globalization espoused by proponents of globalization. Similarly, new books regularly instruct corporations on how to do business in the networked world of social media, while protesters annually resist the empire they see in corporate globalization. These metaphors in themselves are neither right nor wrong. They are ways of thinking about globalization used by millions around the world. And they are ways of studying globalization. Metaphors matter.

A DEFINITION OF GLOBALIZATION

In this last section, I want to conclude our discussion of the language of globalization by offering my own definition. Definitions can seem like a dry topic, so I wanted to start this section with humor. I did a Google search with the keywords *joke*, *definition*, and *globalization*. The first dozen results were the same joke. I am not even sure it is a joke. It is perhaps an example of black humor. Here it is:

QUESTION: What is the truest definition of *globalization*?
ANSWER: Princess Diana's death.
QUESTION: How come?
ANSWER: An English princess with an Egyptian boyfriend crashes in a French tunnel, driving a German car with a Dutch engine, driven by a Belgian who was drunk on Scottish whiskey, followed closely by Italian paparazzi on Japanese motorcycles, and treated by an American doctor using Brazilian medicines!
              That, my friend, is Globalization!

The definition, though somewhat tasteless, does show someone trying to comprehend this troublesome concept. One task remains for this chapter: to offer its own definition of globalization. There might be as many definitions of globalization in the world as there are people. That is not necessarily a bad thing. It simply means that writers or speakers must be clear about what they mean when they talk about globalization. I've already tried to make clear the many assumptions and beliefs that underlie my discussion. I've maintained that historical, political, cultural, and economic forces, now called globalization, have worked in concert with media from the dawn of time to our present day, and that globalization and media—two words that only came into usage in the twentieth century—capture practices that have roots deep in the history of humanity. Humans have always been globalizing, though they have not used that word. And humans have always been communicating with media, though they have not used that word.

Thus, without further ado, my definition: *globalization* is defined as a set of multiple, uneven, and sometimes overlapping historical processes, including economics, politics, and culture, that have combined with the evolution of media technology to create the conditions under which the globe itself can now be understood as "an imagined community."

It is a mouthful, I know. But *globalization* is a mouthful. Here are some of the definition's important parts: Globalization is not one process but multiple processes—economics, politics, and culture. And these processes are not new. They have deep historical roots. And they overlap and influence one another through time. For example, within culture, the rise of Islam had great consequences for politics. In politics, the rise of the British Empire had great consequences worldwide for cultures. All these processes over time—the spread of trade and markets, the rise and fall of empires, the intermingling of cultures—together make up what we now call globalization.

Two other aspects of the definition deserve to be fully explained. I am making a claim that developments in media technology are crucial to globalization. You won't see that in every definition of globalization. People usually recognize that the media are important. But, as you know, I am arguing that media have been, and are, essential to globalization. The following chapter, I hope, will make that case. And, lastly, I am suggesting that the globe itself can be understood as an "imagined community." That is a concept within a long, thoughtful tradition, considered in chapter 4, a tradition that can further enrich our understanding of globalization and media.

3

THE ROLE OF MEDIA
IN GLOBALIZATION

A History

FROM BONGOS TO BLACKBERRYS

In December 1994, a trio of speleologists—cave scientists—were exploring in southern France. Deep within a cave on a limestone cliff, the men were astounded to find on the walls hundreds of intricate, colorful animal paintings. Their astonishment soon increased. Testing showed that the paintings were thirty thousand years old, etched by Upper Paleolithic—Stone Age—people who had first crossed into Europe from Africa. The paintings, in what is now called the Chauvet Cave, named after one of the explorers, are considered some of the oldest known communication *media*. They were painstakingly carved and painted. They were an attempt to record information of predators and prey for the people of that time and times to come. And they were a success. We are still viewing them thirty thousand years later.

The Chauvet Cave paintings are just one example of the deep historical roots of global media, roots that reach back really to the dawn of humankind. From cave paintings to home pages, from smoke signals to satellites, from bongos to Blackberrys, the evolution of media has been essential to human life, has arisen in the context of social life, and has been integral to globalization.

OUT OF AFRICA—WITH MEDIA

Human evolution remains a subject of study and controversy. However, an increasingly dominant view among scientists is that *Homo sapiens*, our ancestors, originated in Africa and migrated out of the area fifty thousand to one hundred thousand years ago. They eventually replaced populations of *Homo erectus* in Asia and *Homo neanderthalensis* in Europe, species that became extinct. *Homo sapiens* survived because of their large, highly developed brains—the name means "wise man" or "knowing man" in Latin—and an erect body carriage that freed the hands and arms. They survived, too, because they created tools and weapons. And they survived, as most species do, because of communication—the ability to attract mates, sound warnings, cry for help, or call the tribe. Our earliest ancestors likely used some form of language, perhaps adapting the intricate calls of chimpanzees. Speech eventually developed. Speech allowed great strides in hunting, gathering, and other acts that needed social cooperation.

The human voice, however, can only carry short distances and has no permanence. The brains and hands of *Homo sapiens* thus also developed means of communicating—media—across space and time. *Homo sapiens* were quite creative. They communicated over distance at first with shouts and songs, then drums and horns, and eventually smoke and fire. They also communicated over time, leaving word for those to come, with tree carvings, wood sculptures, and specially arranged stones, as well as cave paintings. These media were reminders for themselves as well as messages for future generations. The media were used to mark paths to rivers, point out places to hunt, or warn of dangers. These aural and visual devices are the ancestors of our own communication media. And they were key to the early stages of what we now call globalization.

In this chapter, we will trace the development of communication media and show how those media were essential to ongoing processes of globalization. Our starting point: The human impulse to globalize and the human need to communicate over distance have proceeded hand in hand through time. As our ancestors left Africa, they developed and used media of communication that helped them spread across the globe. And the links between globalization and media continue to this day. In many ways, globalization cannot be understood without the study of those media.

We come again to the question raised in our introduction. Did the technology actually shape humanity? Or did humanity shape technology? What will drive the history of globalization and media—technology or humanity? Before studying media technology, we must first grapple with this academic debate over "technological determinism." Some argue that technology has been the most important force shaping human life and determining human conditions. They say that the discovery of new technologies—steam engine, gunpowder, printing press, or computer—immediately alters human life and has been the primary driver of human history.

Many writers who celebrate media and globalization believe in some form of technological determinism. *New York Times* columnist Thomas Friedman, for example, author of *The World Is Flat*, is a cheerful technological determinist. "*I am a technological determinist!*" he writes in italics. "*Guilty as charged.*"[1] You already know my bias. For me, human action and agency—taking place in specific historical, social, political, and cultural circumstances—leads to evolutions in technology. Ultimately, you will want to decide for yourself. Look at the technologies in your own life—from cell phones, computers, television, and video games, to cars, bullet trains, and jet airplanes—do those technologies shape your behavior? Let's look at the argument.

TECHNOLOGY AND SOCIAL CHANGE: THE DEBATE

As we noted, some scholars believe that technology determines human history. The theory of technological determinism says technology advances in predictable ways. It says those technological advances then shape human events. It says technology thus has enormous effects on people and history. This privileging of technology can be traced back at least to the intellectual excitement created by the advances of the Enlightenment in the eighteenth century when humans marveled at, and feared, the growing power and impact of technology and science.

Technological determinists can usually be divided into two camps. Both camps believe in the power of technology to shape human life. Some believe that the effects of technology are beneficial for people and their societies. Marshall McLuhan can be seen as a technological determinist who embraced technology's benefits. He believed that the invention of the alphabet allowed math, science, and philosophy to arise in ancient Greece. He believed that the printing press led to mass literacy, which led to industrialization and the creation of the nation-state. He believed that television led to changes and advances in human perception and understanding.

Other writers share a belief in technological determinism. But they dread its power. In *Technopoly: The Surrender of Culture to Technology*, Neil Postman describes technology as a "dangerous enemy" that destroys the vital sources of our humanity. He argues that "information has become a form of garbage, not only incapable of answering the most fundamental human questions but barely useful in providing coherent direction to the solution of even mundane problems."[2] Similarly, a provocative cover story in *The Atlantic* asked, "Is Google Making Us Stoopid?"[3] The author, Nicholas Carr, followed that up with a book, *The Shallows: What the Internet Is Doing to Our Brains.*[4]

"Social determinism" can be understood as the opposition to technological determinism. Social determinists place their emphasis on people and society, not technology. They do not believe that technology advances in predictable ways. They instead believe that history, society, politics, and economics influence what technologies get created and how they are used. In *Technoculture*, for example, Lelia Green argues that social processes determine technology for social purposes.[5] She says that every technological development throughout history, including media technology, came from a social need, primarily economic, political, or military. Power comes into the discussion here as well. Developing technology costs money. Social determinists often study how the development of technology is driven by powerful actors—such as corporations or foundations—or government institutions, such as the military.

Here is a simple example of the debate between technological and social determinists using the iPod, the ubiquitous digital music player. Technological determinists might say that the iPod developed predictably. Audio devices continually got smaller and cheaper, from the big box radio and large record player to the transistor radio to the stereo cassette player to the portable cassette player to the Walkman to the iPod. And technological determinists would say that the creation of the iPod has shaped the way people listen to music, from bedrooms to cars to gymnasiums. Social determinists might say that the iPod was developed by Steve Jobs and Apple to advance in a market first created by Sony Walkman. The technology was planned to meet people's increasing desire for portable music collections—and Apple's desire to make large profits. And Apple's genius for designing products led to a huge financial and technological success.

As with many such debates, no right or wrong answer exists. Both sides can be right. Writers—and readers—just need to consider the issue and the play between humans and technology. Any study of media and globalization, especially, should make clear its approach to technology. This book will chart a middle path and not be reduced or confined to either of the determinist camps, though its sympathies lie with social determinists. Like social determinists, I believe that historical, social, political, and economic forces have had, and will have, tremendous influence on the creation and the use of media. Like technological determinists, however, I believe that particular—and often unanticipated—attributes of a particular medium do shape how humans use the technology and do have large social effects.

The Internet offers a good example of how this approach to technology and social change might work. Much of the motivation and funding for computer and network research that led to the Internet came from a very powerful political actor—the U.S. military, particularly the U.S. Department of Defense. In the 1950s, the height of the Cold War between the United States and the Soviet Union, the military was worried that a bomb hitting Washington or New York could wipe out U.S. information and communication capacities. The military was interested in the ability of computers to move and store information among multiple locations on a network so that a military strike at any one point in the country would not be devastating. Certainly social determinists can point to the historical, political, social, and economic forces at work in the creation of computer networks.

However, the resulting technology—the Internet—has particular attributes that have led it to develop in ways unimagined by the military. The technology is open ended. With Tim Berners-Lee's later invention of the World Wide Web, the Internet burst national boundaries and went global. The technology is relatively cheap. It spread quickly to many different organizations and classes, not just military researchers or academic elites. The technology is interactive. Its communication and networking capacities were explosively successful, giving rise to Facebook, MySpace, blogs, online political action groups, and many more. The technology is archival. Its storage capacities have allowed governments, universities, libraries, museums, and others to change how they store, retrieve, and display information. Certainly technological determinists can say that the very nature of Internet technology has shaped culture in innumerable ways.

Neither technological nor social determinism can capture the birth and growth of the Internet, or any other media. The trajectory of media technology is powerful. Yet equally powerful are the governments, groups, corporations, and individuals who have created and employed media to globalize the world. This understanding of both technological and social determinism provides an important backdrop for the study of media and globalization across the span of human evolution. From the drums of ancient Africa to the Internet, a history of media and globalization will benefit from attention to predictable advances in technology and the attributes of individual media as well as to the social, political, and economic contexts from which the media arise and in which they are used.

EVOLUTION OF MEDIA AND GLOBALIZATION

Scholars have found it logical and helpful to organize the historical study of media by time periods or stages. Each period is characterized by its dominant medium. For example, the Canadian theorist Harold Innis, Marshall

McLuhan's teacher, writing in the 1940s and 1950s, divided media into three periods: oral, print, and electronic.[6] James Lull, writing at the close of the twentieth century, added digital to those three.[7] Terhi Rantanen places script before the printing press and breaks down the electronic period into wired and wireless, for six periods.[8] I find that five time periods usefully captures the study of globalization and media: oral, script, print, electronic, and digital.

Media scholars use such demarcations to make larger points about those time periods. Innis was interested in how different media shaped societies' views on time and space. Oral cultures, he said, lack permanent media and have a bias for time over space. The printing press, he said, provided more permanent media, such as books, and gave rise to societies that favored space over time, which eventually led them to expand and seek control over space, giving rise to empires. Other scholars too, such as Lull and Rantanen, look at how different time periods and their media have shaped the lives of individuals as well as their societies.

Our purpose will be somewhat similar. We will look at the different time periods—oral, script, print, electronic, and digital—and point out how the media of each time period contributed to the globalization of our world. This somewhat systematic accounting isolates and highlights the essential role of media in globalization over time and, I hope, firmly establishes the centrality of media for future studies of globalization. However, it is important to stress that I do not see globalization or media proceeding—or advancing—along an inevitable, inexorable path of *progress*. Media—and globalization as well—have developed sporadically, erratically, in fits and starts, driven by human needs, desires, and actions, resulting in great benefits and sometimes greater harm. Charting history is not necessarily charting progress. The history of media and globalization is the history of humanity itself.

ORAL COMMUNICATION

Humans spread out and covered the globe largely through the use of one medium: the iPod. Only kidding. Speech is often the most overlooked medium in histories of globalization. Yet the oral medium—human speech—is the oldest and most enduring of all media. Over hundreds and thousands of years, despite numerous changes undergone by humans and their societies, the very first and last humans will share at least one thing—the ability to speak. We rightly are interested in how globalization has been shaped by the printing press, electronic media such as television and film, and digital media such as computers and cell phones. However, speech has been with us at for least two hundred thousand years, script for less than seven thousand years, print for less than six hundred years, and digital technology for less than fifty years.

Our ancestors, *Homo sapiens*, survived because of their ability to speak. Even at its most primitive level, speech allowed humans to work together as individuals or within social groups. When speech developed into language, *Homo sapiens* had developed a medium that would set them apart from every other species and allow them to cover and conquer the world.[9]

How did the medium of language aid globalization? Language allowed humans to cooperate. During a hunt, the ability to coordinate was a considerable advantage. And there were other advantages: Sharing information about land, water, climate, and weather aided humans' ability to travel and adapt to different environments. Sharing information about tools and weapons led to the spread of technology. Humans eventually moved to every corner of the world, encountering new environments and experiences at each turn. Language was their most important tool.

Language helped humans move, but it also helped them settle down. Human settlements are a relatively recent phenomenon in the history of *Homo sapiens*. Through most of history, humans lived in small nomadic groups, hunting and gathering across the land. Probably around 8000 BCE, humans settled in the Fertile Crescent in the Middle East, domesticated animals, and planted crops.[10] More permanent and secure settlements followed. Language played a part here as well. It stored and transmitted important agricultural information across time as one generation passed on its knowledge to the next. It also allowed the creation of other villages and towns as humans shared information about fertile locations and surroundings.

Language also led to markets and the trade of goods and services. At the local level, people might exchange fish or meat for fruits or vegetables. Such practices grew into trade between cities and regions and eventually into cross-continental trade routes—built on the language of bartering and haggling. These organized, permanent trading centers grew and multiplied, giving rise to cities.

Even across great distances, information was shared through language. Town criers, traveling minstrels, and fleet-footed messengers aided communication. Eventually systems of beacons, torches, flares, and mirrors helped spread messages over many miles, but the human voice still was crucial. L. H. Samuelson studied the Zulu's message system, which was handed down over centuries. He called it "human wireless telegraphy."

The Zulus are celebrated for being marvelous news-carriers, and Europeans have often been astonished to find how swiftly news travels in their country, without the aid of paper, letters or telegrams. Whatever takes place is known for miles and, in an incredibly short time,—what happens in the morning is known everywhere, long before sunset.[11]

Linked by such communication, cities continued to grow in size. And perhaps around 4000 BCE, humans' first civilization was created at Sumer in the Middle East. Sometimes called the "cradle of civilization," Sumer is thought to be the birthplace of the wheel, plow, irrigation, and *writing*.

SCRIPT

The invention of writing may have occurred in a number of civilizations, such as Sumer, Egypt, and China. Some histories of media technology skip over this stage or give it brief mention as a transition between oral cultures and cultures of the printing press. But the more I study the history of script, the more convinced I become that this era was crucial for globalization and media. Language was essential but imperfect. Distance causes trouble for oral communication. It takes elaborate systems to communicate with language over great expanses. Time also causes trouble. Language relies on human memory, which is limited in capacity and not always perfect. Script—the very first writing—allowed humans to communicate and share knowledge and ideas over much larger spaces and across much longer times.

Writing has its own evolution and developed from cave paintings, petroglyphs, and hieroglyphs.[12] Early writing systems began to appear after 3000 BCE, with symbols carved into clay tablets to keep account of trade. These "cuneiform" marks later developed into symbols that represented the syllables of languages and eventually led to the creation of alphabets, the scripted letters that represent the smallest sounds of a language. These alphabets, learned now in preschools around the world, were central to the evolution of humankind and its civilizations.

But script needed to be written on something. Writing *surfaces* even had their own evolution. Writing was done at first as carvings into wood, clay, bronze, bones, stone, and even tortoise shells. Scientists have found various fragments of writing on clay tablets, shells, and stones that date back to 3000 BCE. Around the same time, ancient Egypt created one of the most popular writing surfaces—papyrus (from which the English word *paper* eventually derived). Created from a plant found along the lower Nile River, Egyptians found that they could peel and slice papyrus into sheets on which they could write. Papyrus greatly aided the ease of creating and transporting writing. It certainly was easier to carry papyrus than tortoise shells. And the use of papyrus spread in civilizations throughout the Mediterranean region. Parchment, created from animal skins, was found to bring similar results.

With script on papyrus and parchment, humans had a medium that catapulted globalization. Assyrian, Phoenician, Egyptian, Greek, and other civilizations used papyrus and parchment to maintain and extend their cultures over larger and larger expanses. The trading systems, laws, religious practices, military decrees, and numerous other dimensions of economic, cultural, and political life were enhanced by the medium of script. Civilizations were able to grow into empires.

The Roman Empire—a paragon of globalization—in particular used papyrus to expand its global grasp. Rome controlled Egypt, the source of papyrus. It thus was easily able to publish various *acta*, such as *Acta senatus*, the activities of the Senate, which had wide circulation. Julius Caesar is credited with publishing the first newspaper, the *Acta diurna populi*, or *Acta diurna*, the daily political and social events of the day. Copies were written by hand on papyrus and posted around Rome and its provinces.

"Writing became the medium of choice for relating news over distances," says Mitchell Stephens in his history of news. "Rome's dominions stretched over great distances, and unlike Alexander's empire, Rome was able to develop a system of written news equal of the task of traversing them."[13] Information on wars, uprisings, markets, cultures, deaths, marriages, and other news thus circulated through the empire, which once extended from Egypt to Scotland.

The creation of paper was undoubtedly the most important advance in the history of writing. Scholars have actually found agreement on a very precise year for its invention—105 CE.[14] Archaeological evidence from that year shows an official report to the emperor during the Chinese Han dynasty. The report proclaimed the invention of paper by Ts'ai Lun. Made from tree bark beaten into pulp, paper was lightweight, easy to produce, and plentiful in supply, unlike papyrus. Like Rome, now able to support a vast empire, the Han dynasty spread across much of Asia and lasted from 200 BCE to after 200 CE. Papermaking spread even farther, reaching throughout Asia, the Islamic world, and after a thousand years eventually into Europe.

The age of writing and script too often gets overlooked in histories of media technology. Yet, as we have seen, script was critically important to the emergence, maintenance, and growth of the human civilizations and empires that fueled globalization. These large human communities had many of the social structures and groupings that exist today—laws, codes, divisions of labor, protocols, distinct armies and militias, social classes, priestly elders, and ruling officials. It would have been difficult, if not impossible, to hold such societies together and have them persist through time with the impermanence of oral language. Script allowed for the written and permanent codification of economic, cultural, religious, and political practice. These codes could then be spread out over great distances and handed down through time. The great civilizations, from Egypt and Greece to Rome and China, were made possible through script. If globalization is considered the economic, cultural, and political integration of the world and its people, then surely script—the written word—must be considered an essential medium.

THE PRINTING PRESS

It started the "information revolution" and transformed markets, businesses, nations, schools, churches, governments, armies, and more. All histories of media and globalization acknowledge the great role of the printing press. Many *begin* with the printing press. It's easy to see why.

Prior to the printing press, the production and copying of written documents was slow, cumbersome, and expensive. The papyrus, parchment, and paper that spread civilizations were the province of a select, powerful few. Reading and writing, too, were practices of the ruling and religious elite. The rich and powerful controlled information. With the advent of the printing press, reading material suddenly was cheaply made and easily circulated. Millions of books, pamphlets, and flyers were produced, reproduced, and circulated. Literacy followed, and the literacy of common people was to revolutionize every aspect of life. The explosive flow of economic, cultural, and political ideas around the world connected and changed people and cultures in ways never before possible. Truly, the processes of globalization were inextricably linked to the development of the printing press.[15]

Johannes Gutenberg is often credited with inventing the printing press around 1450 in Germany. However, perhaps unsurprisingly, China, the birthplace of paper, had seen other kinds of printing presses for centuries before. In China, woodblocks were used to create pages of text, and in 1040 movable woodblocks were in place. Gutenberg's great invention was a press that used movable *metal* type. (Interestingly, a very similar press was invented in Korea around the same time.) Gutenberg's press was efficient, fast, durable, and easy to replicate. "What was revolutionary about Gutenberg's printing press was how much more could be produced, more quickly and cheaply than by hand," says communication scholar Elizabeth Hanson.[16] Printing presses were rapidly established across Europe.

In a masterful, two-volume, 750-page treatise, historian Elizabeth Eisenstein surveyed the many profound influences of the printing press.[17] Her findings range across the Enlightenment, the Protestant Reformation, the scientific revolution, and more. Two overarching consequences, however, can be suggested from her work. First, the printing press changed the very nature of knowledge. It preserved knowledge, which had been more malleable in oral cultures. It also standardized knowledge, which had become more variable as it spread orally across regions and lands. Script and papyrus had begun the process of preservation and standardization, but not nearly to the extent allowed by printing presses.

A second consequence: print encouraged the challenge of political and religious authority because of its ability to circulate competing views. Eisenstein notes that "fear of disapproval, a sense of isolation, the force of local community sanctions, the habit of respectful submission to traditional authority—all might be weakened."[18] The printing press reconfigured power and people. For centuries in Europe, the monks and priests of the Catholic Church were among the few with the education, time, and resources for reading and writing books. The Church thus had a kind of monopoly over knowledge. Church officials could decide what the illiterate public should know. The printing press, however, encouraged the literacy of the public and the growth of schools. It also allowed for the publication and circulation of views that dissented from the Church. As we saw in the introductory chapter, Martin Luther posted his Ninety-Five Theses critiquing the Church in 1517, a little more than fifty years after the invention of the printing press. The resulting Protestant Reformation would reshape world religions and politics.

We can find other influences of the printing press on globalization. The printing press, for example, led to the elevation of a few, select languages across the globe—*national* languages, which helped give rise to modern *nations*. Previously, most lands were divided into numerous regions with their own oral dialects and vernacular languages. Printers, however, could select only one language for a publication. They strove for the largest sales and often chose the most common language. People who wanted to read had to learn that version of the language, helping it to become even more common. The eventual creation of a national language offered people a shared sense of identity and of belonging to a group. The publication of shared social, cultural, and political materials furthered that sense of identity. In the decades after the printing press, modern nations were born.[19]

The printing press also greatly aided scientific advancement. More people were literate and schooled. More people could pursue research. Too, researchers, inventors, and scientists had previously worked with little awareness of other, perhaps related work being done around the world or even in their own region. Publication and reports of research and inventions allowed scientists to share and then build upon knowledge. The scientific revolution of the sixteenth century, which saw advances in biology, physics, astronomy, chemistry, and other subjects, can be directly tied to the printing press.

In other ways as well, the medium of the printing press was central to the shaping and development of the world. The rise of inexpensive, easily obtained magazines and daily newspapers brought news from around the world to people. People increasingly learned of lands and cultures far from where they could travel. They learned about the world. Truly, the printing press helped foster globalization—and knowledge of globalization.

ELECTRONIC MEDIA

In January 2010, *Avatar*, directed by James Cameron, became the top money-making film of all time. It grossed $1.86 billion worldwide in just thirty-nine days, a figure that continues to climb. The previous record holder was *Titanic*, also directed by Cameron. No wonder that Cameron, after winning an Oscar, exultantly quoted a line from *Titanic*: "I'm king of the world!"

Film has indeed conquered the world as one of the most powerful forms of mass media created during the last two centuries. Beginning in the nineteenth century, a host of new media, including film, would revolutionize the ongoing processes of globalization. Scholars have come to group and call these "electronic media" because they require electromagnetic energy—electricity—to use. The telegraph, telephone, radio, film, and television are the usual media collected under electronic media. Many volumes have been produced that explore the tremendous global economic, social, cultural, and political impact of these media. Conversely, scholars have explored how globalization has shaped them, as in the study of the globalization of the film industry. The vast reach of these electronic media continues to open up new vistas in the economic, political, and cultural processes of globalization. Only a brief summary is possible here.

In our modern world, the telegraph is not thought of as a revolutionary medium. But in its time, the telegraph was a sensation with great consequences. Samuel F. B. Morse began work on a machine in the 1830s that could send coded messages—dots and dashes—over electrical lines.

By 1844, he could communicate instantaneously over a line stretched between Baltimore and Washington, D.C. Long-distance communication was transformed.

Why? The word helps explain: In Greek, *tele* is "far," and *graph* is "write." The telegraph could "write far" and effectively separated communication and transportation. Previously, most information, including print, traveled only at the speed of man on a horse or train. Now communication could travel at the speed of light. Within ten years, twenty-three thousand miles of telegraph wire was strung across the country. The effects were enormous. Almost immediately, rail travel was more efficient and safe since information about arrivals or delays could be passed down the line ahead of the trains. Corporations and businesses were able to exchange information about markets and prices. Newspapers could report information instantaneously. The telegraph also aided the development of the West, since communication no longer took days or weeks. By 1866, a transatlantic cable was laid between the United States and Europe, and the telegraph became a truly global medium. The volume of international trade jumped exponentially. Governments and scientists, too, exchanged information over the wires, which eventually circled the world.

Media scholar James Carey captured the often overlooked impact of the telegraph. He wrote,

> A thorough treatment of the consequences of the telegraph would attempt to demonstrate how this instrument altered the spatial and temporal boundaries of human interaction, brought into existence new forms of language as well as new conceptual systems, and brought about new structures of social relations, particularly by fostering a national commercial middle class.[20]

The ability to transmit speech over distance was the next communication breakthrough. Though not always considered a mass medium, the telephone surely contributed further to connecting the world. Alexander Graham Bell is credited with inventing the telephone in 1876. It quickly became a globally adopted medium. Bell himself made the first long-distance call, to Canada, in 1876. By 1927, the first transatlantic call was made via radio.

The creation of the cell phone in 1973 was especially crucial in the context of globalization and media. Relatively cheap to produce and buy, and easy to learn and transport, cell phones have quickly become the world's dominant communication device. They have penetrated even the world's most remote regions and villages. In Africa, for example, which has poor infrastructure for wired technology, close to 80 percent of the people have cell phones. Indeed, according to the International Telecommunication Union, Africa became the first continent where the number of mobile phone users exceeded those using wired lines.[21] It supports the commerce and trade of farmers and fishermen; makes possible microfinance; allows for communication among government, aid groups, and villages; and helps communicate vital health information. As new tools and applications continue to be developed, the cell phone may become one of the most transformative media of our time.

Radio developed alongside the telegraph and telephone in the late 1890s. The technology was first conceived to be used as a "wireless telegraph." By the early 1900s, speech indeed was being transmitted without wires. By the 1920s, broadcast stations were "on the air," transmitting music and news. Radio quickly became a global medium, reaching the most distant regions without the construction of wires or roads.[22] Different support systems were established. Companies that produced and sold radios owned many of the early radio stations, which were vehicles to sell more radios. In the United States, radio stations came to be supported mostly by advertising; in Great Britain, support came from the government.[23]

Regardless of the support, in every country, radio eventually became a potent globalizing force, instantaneously bringing news and entertainment from around the world into villages and homes. For much of the twentieth century, radio was the only mass medium available in many remote villages. Radio was crucially involved with the upheavals of globalization during the twentieth century, from radio broadcasts that riveted audiences during World War II, to the propaganda services that did battle worldwide during the Cold War, to the so-called death radio that helped drive the genocide of Tutsi in Rwanda.[24] The ability of radio to broadcast over the Internet has only expanded its global reach.

As we have seen, the early decades of the 1900s were especially fertile for the creation of what was coming to be known as "mass media." Along with the telegraph, telephone, and radio, film arose as another potent medium. Silent motion pictures were shown as early as the 1870s. But as a mass medium, film developed in the 1890s. *The Great Train Robbery*, made in 1903, is often credited as the first narrative film, ten minutes long with fourteen scenes. Film soon developed into an artistic medium of great cultural expression. By the 1920s, directors such as D. W. Griffith, Sergei Eisenstein, F. W. Murnau, and Fritz Lang were using film to capture powerful narratives that resonated within and across cultures. The worldwide success of films such as *Avatar* and *Titanic* offers resounding examples of the confluence of globalization and media. Though Hollywood and Bollywood get much attention, the cultivation of film industries in nations around the globe continues to this day.[25]

For many people, television is considered the most powerful and pervasive mass medium yet created. Though television programming existed back in the 1920s, the years after World War II saw the explosion in the production and penetration of television into homes around the world. The astounding growth of television in the United States is well documented. According to the U.S. Census Bureau's *Statistical Abstract*, before 1950, less than 10 percent of U.S. homes had televisions. In five years, the number grew to 64.5 percent. By 1960, 87.1 percent of U.S. homes had television. Worldwide growth was rapid too. By the end of the 1960s, half the countries in the world had television stations.

Television brought together the visual and aural power of film with the accessibility of radio: People sat in their living rooms and kitchens and viewed pictures and stories from across the globe. The world was brought into the home. The amount, range, and intensity of communication with other lands and cultures occurred in ways simply not possible before. For some scholars, the introduction of television was a defining moment in globalization. As we have seen, Marshall McLuhan proclaimed the world a "global village," largely because of television. Scholars from every discipline have acknowledged its globalizing powers. Cultural anthropologist Arjun Appadurai describes a "rupture" in social relations caused by the intersection of migration and electronic media, especially television. He says that these media, on a scale unknown before, allowed people to see new worlds and thus imagine a different life for themselves.[26] Sociologist Anthony Giddens, too, has emphasized how television and other electronic media have intensified the speed and scope of interactions among people around the world.[27]

Television became even more powerful with cable. Students always roll their eyes when I begin sentences with "when I was growing up." The phrase reminds them of lectures from their parents. But when I was growing up, we had three network television stations and two local stations—we were in New York, so we had those extra two local stations, unknown to many communities. Cable television changed all that. Cable brought a plethora of channels and choices to television. The vast number of channels led to the creation of niche channels devoted to topics such as history, weather, golf, and travel. Some of those niche channels for news, music, and sports now epitomize the modern era of globalization: CNN, MTV, and ESPN. For example, MTV International is seen in more than two dozen countries, each with its own mix of local and global music. That was not possible—when I was growing up.

DIGITAL MEDIA

Digital media are most often electronic media that rely on digital codes— the long arcane combinations of 0s and 1s that represent information. Many of our earlier media, such as phones and televisions, can now be considered digital. Indeed, digital may even be blurring the lines among media. If you can watch television, take photographs, show movies, and send e-mail on your smart phone, what does that mean for our neat categorization of media into television, film, or phone?

The computer, though, is the usual representation of digital media. The computer comes as the latest and some would argue most significant medium to influence globalization. You likely are aware of the many ways that computers have contributed to globalization. In the realm of economics, computers allow instantaneous, global trading twenty-four hours a day. Anyone with a computer has access to economic information that just a few years ago was in the hands of a wealthy few. Too, computers have revolutionized work in every industry and trade. They streamline tasks, open up new areas and methods of research, and allow any company or industry access to a global marketplace. Some of the largest companies in the world, such as Microsoft, Apple, Google, Facebook, and more, arose in the digital era and have been instrumental to globalization.

In the realm of politics, computers allow citizens access to information from around the world, even information that governments would like to conceal. For example, the Chinese government strives mightily to prevent its people from learning of the 1989 crackdown on protesters at Tiananmen Square. The effort often fails because blogs, social media, Twitter, text messaging, and more allow citizens to communicate among themselves. The 2009 elections in Iran gave rise to what some called "the Twitter Revolution" because protesters used Twitter and social networking sites to communicate with each other while disputing the victory of Iranian president Mahmoud Ahmadinejad. As we saw in the introduction, the people of Tunisia and Egypt overthrew dictators in what were called "Facebook revolutions."

However, computers are not always benign political actors. They also allow government access to large amounts of private information and permit unprecedented surveillance. In 2010, Google shut down some of its services in China because of demands for censorship. Google also said some of its data had been compromised, including the e-mail of Chinese activists.[28] Also in 2010, after WikiLeaks published sensitive and classified U.S. diplomatic cables, U.S. authorities wanted to indict WikiLeaks founder Julian Assange and sought his Twitter and social media communications for use in prosecution.[29]

And computers have transformed cultural life. Access to information around the globe allows people to adopt and adapt new practices in music, sports, education, religion, fashion, cuisine, the arts, and other areas of culture. People talk with friends, relations, and even strangers around the world through Skype, Google Chat, and other programs. Immigration has been changed in fundamental ways. Immigrants now can remain in daily contact with friends and family in the home country and have ready access to home media. Every professional sport—from football (American and global) to baseball to cricket to basketball—strives for a global audience. Religion too has seen the influence of digital media. In the virtual world, *Second Life*, in which close to seven million people engage in virtual lives, religion figures prominently. Churches, mosques, and synagogues have been set up to attract a virtual faithful. Life Church, an evangelical denomination, offers Sunday services simultaneously in its Oklahoma site and in *Second Life*.[30] As we will see in a later chapter, the confluence of globalization with local cultures has produced intense controversy as well as magnificent creations.

ONCE AGAIN: NO GLOBALIZATION WITHOUT MEDIA

I will repeat this subhead from the introduction to confirm one of my primary points. The purpose of this chapter has been to track the development of communication media over time and show how those media were essential to the ongoing processes of globalization. Our starting point was that the human impulse to globalize and the human need to communicate over distance have proceeded together through time, each driving and influencing the other. Even in a condensed, chapter-long summary, the partnership of globalization and media is clear. Each of the eras—oral, script, print, electronic, and digital—saw marked influences of media on globalization. It is difficult to imagine globalization occurring without the media that are so crucial to human life.

I have alluded more than once to one of the most important consequences of communication media for globalization. Through media, the people of the world came to know of the world. In a very real sense, media affected the "imagination" of the world, allowing people to imagine a world, a different world from where they were, but a world perhaps accessible and reachable. Such influence on the imagination of the world is terribly important. A "global imaginary" has been necessary for globalization to continue apace. The "global imaginary," though, may also be responsible for suspicion and hostility toward globalization when "globalization does not keep its promises." It is the subject of the next chapter.

4

"THE RISE OF THE GLOBAL IMAGINARY"

The Global Village

THE BLUE MARBLE

Its official title is AS17-148-22727. Its unofficial title is *The Blue Marble*. It is a color photograph of the Earth shot from the Apollo 17 spacecraft in December 1972. Taken from eighteen thousand miles in space, the photograph depicts the blue and white sphere of the planet suspended in the black expanse of the universe. NASA, the U.S. National Aeronautics and Space Administration, allowed the photograph to enter the public domain and now estimates that it may be the most widely distributed image in history. "We went to explore the Moon," said Eugene Cernan, commander of the flight, "and in fact discovered the Earth."[1]

This chapter looks at one of the crucial but sometimes overlooked dimensions of globalization and media. Globalization is made possible by the work of the *imagination*. That is, people have needed to be able to truly imagine the world—and imagine themselves acting in the world—for globalization to proceed. And the media—which bring stories, pictures, sights, and sounds from other peoples and places, even outer space—often have been the means by which the imagination of the world has been made possible. *The Blue Marble* is just one of the many ways by which media allow humankind to imagine the world.

People today perhaps take "the world" for granted. We all know that, with enough money, we can hop on a plane and go anywhere, or make a transcontinental phone call, or use Google or Wikipedia to find photographs and information on even the most remote places. That imagination, however, was a long time coming for humankind. For centuries, many parts of the world were unknown to other parts of the world. People told fantastic stories of these other places. They told stories of primitive villages and fearful savages. They told stories of unfathomable wealth and streets made of gold. They could not imagine what life was like elsewhere.

As Arjun Appadurai has argued, the imagination is not a trifling fantasy but a "social fact." The imagination is a "staging ground for action."[2] The Irish people, starving from a potato famine in the 1800s, *imagined* a better life in America, and millions emigrated. The Egyptian people, suffering under a dictatorship, *imagined* a better life for themselves in 2011. They filled Tahrir Square in Cairo, overthrew the dictator, and realized their imagination. The imagination—in the context of globalization and media—can be an especially fertile concept for study.

We will start our study with *the imaginary*, a term that scholars often use, and one that has enriched research in numerous fields. We will look at the ways theorists have employed the imaginary in study of how individuals, nations, and societies imagine themselves and the world.[3] Then we will look at the role of media. In this perspective, the media have not only physically linked the globe with cables, broadband, and wireless networks, but have also linked the globe with stories, images, myths, and metaphors. The media are helping to bring about a fundamentally new imaginary, what scholar Manfred Steger has called a rising *global imaginary*—the globe itself as imagined community. In the past, only a few, privileged people thought of themselves as "cosmopolitan"—citizens of the world. Cosmopolitanism, I argue, is now a feature of modern life. People imagine themselves as part of the world.

What are the implications of this global imaginary? Here we will return to media scholar Marshall McLuhan. The global imaginary surely seems like a modern notion. But in the 1960s, McLuhan anticipated this phenomenon with his conception of the global village. The global village, McLuhan felt, would bring about a utopia. Drawn closely together by media, people would be like neighbors. From its introduction, though, the global village has been a source of controversy. We will look at the global village debate, with particular attention to a critique offered by the historian of technology and science Lewis Mumford. Years before McLuhan, with strikingly similar language, Mumford too found utopian hope in media technology. He too hoped for a villagelike world of community and grace. However, Mumford watched with dismay as media technology was used instead for capitalism, militarism, profit, and power. His dreams became nightmares. Mumford's later work savaged the possibility of the global village and railed against its implications. Mumford became one of McLuhan's most ferocious critics.

Ultimately, however, this chapter will argue that globalization and media are producing a macabre marriage of the visions of Mumford and

McLuhan. The dawning global imaginary is the realization of McLuhan's global village. As McLuhan predicted, media and globalization have connected the world and its people from end to end so that we can indeed imagine the world as a village. However, the connection, closeness, and interdependence of the global village have brought no collective harmony or peace. Instead, we will conclude, globalization and media are combining to create the dark, dystopian world that Mumford dreaded. We will thus arrive at the construct we need to proceed: the global village of Babel.

STUDY OF THE IMAGINARY

People have long used *imaginary* as an adjective to describe imagined beings or objects, such as imaginary friends or imaginary selves. It makes sense that a psychiatrist would be intrigued by the imaginary. The French psychoanalyst and social theorist Jacques Lacan took special interest in this process.[4] His psychoanalytic system is rich, intricate, and difficult to distill. Yet much of his work has had great influence in philosophy, critical studies, literary theory, and other arenas. Unlike many Freudian analysts, Lacan does not place his primary focus on the unconscious. Instead, Lacan, who was heavily influenced by Marx, emphasizes the impact of society and culture on people and their psyches.

He argues that people perceive the world in three ways, or orders—the imaginary, the symbolic, and the real.[5] For Lacan, the imaginary is perception shaped by images, imagination, illusion, and, in particular, fantasy. For example, Lacan discusses the fantasies a person builds around a perceived, imagined self and says that the person "ends up by recognizing that this being has never been anything more than his construct in the imaginary and that this construct disappoints all his certainties."[6] For Lacan, then, the imaginary largely is illusion, through Marx, and fantasy, through Freud. The imaginary is a way in which individuals deceive and are deceived, in which they alienate and are alienated.

Cornelius Castoriadis, a Greek philosopher and economist, shared much intellectual kinship with Lacan. Also a social theorist and psychoanalyst, influenced too by Marx and Freud, as well as by Lacan, Castoriadis nevertheless argues for a much different understanding of the imaginary. In *The Imaginary Institution of Society*, Castoriadis extends the imaginary from the individual to society.[7]

He believes that groups of people share imaginings—a social imaginary—that capture essential values and beliefs of the people. The ancient Jews' understandings of the Old Testament God are a social imaginary, Castoriadis says. The Jews believed in that God, who could be stern and unforgiving as well as munificent and kind. That shared belief is a social imaginary. Another example would be the political and philosophical structure established and accepted by the ancient Greeks.[8] Ultimately, societies need social imaginaries for unity and cohesion. In an important line, Castoriadis notes that a social imaginary gives people and society an understanding of their place in the world—"an original investment by society of the world and itself with meaning." And, he says, the social imaginary specifies "a particular importance and particular place in the universe constituted by a given society."[9] I like that line. I think the changes wrought by globalization and media are causing numerous societies, from the United States to China to Egypt to Afghanistan to France, to consider their importance and place in the universe.

As a political scientist, Benedict Anderson has interests different from psychoanalysts and social theorists. Anderson's primary focus is on the origin of nations and nationalism.[10] His question is great. He wonders how a group of people, though spread across vast expanses of land, come to conceive of themselves as a "nation." He points out that "the nation" is a relatively modern idea, developed in the late eighteenth century to replace monarchies and religious empires.[11] Yet, within a fairly short amount of time, people began to see themselves vividly as part of a nation. People's loyalty and dedication to the nation became so strong that they would kill and die for it. How does such a belief take hold?

Anderson's answer, like the psychoanalysts, leads him to the imagination. He says that nations are the result of "imagined communities," a concept now used regularly throughout the humanities and social sciences. People will never meet face to face with all or even most of the other members of their nation, Anderson says, but they can *imagine* themselves as one; "in the minds of each lives the image of their communion."[12]

This imaginary, Anderson theorizes, comes about largely through the media, or, more specifically for Anderson's historical analysis, "print-capitalism."[13] As we saw in our discussion of the printing press, publishers of books, newspapers, and magazines, looking for the largest audiences, print their materials in a common vernacular and make them accessible across the land. Readers who might be divided by local dialects are brought together around a common print language—and common topics. People become aware of other people, places, and events in their own nation. They are aware that others are reading and responding to the same things. They begin to understand themselves as a nation and see differences between their nation and others. Anderson concludes that print capitalism "created the possibility of a new form of imagined community," which set the stage for the modern nation.[14]

The Canadian philosopher Charles Taylor found Anderson's concept enormously useful for his own scholarship on people's understandings of society and social relations.[15] Though interested in the construction of society, not the nation, Taylor draws upon Anderson and proposes, with language similar to Castoriadis', that *modern social imaginaries* are the ways in which people conceive their societies. "I speak of *imaginary* because I'm talking about the way ordinary people 'imagine' their social surroundings, and this is often not expressed in theoretical terms; it is carried in images, stories, and legends."[16]

Taylor's conception differs somewhat from Castoriadis', whose focus is on the dominant imaginary of the group. Taylor's focus is on the beliefs and practices of average people in daily life. He says, "Our social imaginary at any given time is complex. It incorporates a sense of the normal expectations that we have of one another, the kind of common understanding which enables us to carry out the collective practices that make up our social life. This incorporates some sense of how we all fit together in carrying out the common practice."[17] Surely that nice phrase—"how we all fit together"—gets richly complicated in the context of globalization. Who, precisely, is "we"?

THE GLOBAL IMAGINARY: THE WORLD AS IMAGINED COMMUNITY

The imaginary, thus far, has been used by these theorists to understand how individuals and societies imagine themselves and the world. In Castoriadis' words, the imaginary captures the "particular importance and particular place in the universe constituted by a given society."[18] Globalization, however, seems to call for new understandings and new imaginings. Indeed, sociologist Roland Robertson defines globalization in part as "the intensification of consciousness of the world as a whole."[19] Anthony Giddens, too, speaks of "the intensification of worldwide social relations."[20]

People increasingly work, act, study, communicate, and move around the globe. It is the world, rather than the village or state, that becomes their frame of reference. In Taylor's terms, "the sense of how we all fit together" is increasingly becoming global. "We" may actually now mean the people of the world. Yet is this new? Actually, no. The feeling of working, acting, and belonging to the world did not arise in our era of globalization. In other eras, globalization awakened similar impulses. Privileged people called "cosmopolitans"—literally from the Greek, *kosmopolitēs*, citizen of the cosmos—were those who had traveled and perhaps studied abroad, had knowledge of other people and lands, and felt themselves part of the larger world.

Two differences, however, mark our era of globalization. The first difference, alluded to by Robertson and Giddens, is the intensification or intensity of the understanding and consciousness of the world. We can see vividly and instantly into every corner of the world. Communication media are central to this intensification. The power and scope of mass media now bring the world to our living rooms and desktops. The tools of interactive communication, such as cell phones and the Internet, allow regular communication and communion with others around the globe. In our era, we feel more intensely the closeness of the world. The second difference is the expansion and acceleration of global social, economic, and political relations. Acts of globalization have been going on for centuries. However, because of the spread and growth of communication technology, as well as lower costs for travel and technology and rising incomes in many areas of the world, more people than ever are participating in global activities.

Being cosmopolitan is thus no longer a rare attribute but a marked feature of modern life. The immigrant, study-abroad student, account executive, pilot, poet, tourist, and many others feel themselves *of the world*. Can we therefore speak of an emerging global imaginary?

As we have seen, Arjun Appadurai, a cultural anthropologist, argues that new advances and possibilities in media and migration indeed have caused a "rupture" in social relations that allows for new ways of imagining ourselves and the world. He writes that "electronic mediation and mass migration mark the world of the present not as technically new forces but as ones that seem to impel (and sometimes compel) the work of the imagination."[21]

Appadurai realizes of course that media and migration are not new, that not everyone has access to new media, and that not everyone migrates. Yet, he says, the explosive expansion and commingling of media and migration are new. Few people are untouched by advances in media, and few people do not have a friend, relative, or coworker who has come back and forth from distant lands. The work of the imagination now takes place in this global context and becomes "a space of contestation in which individuals and groups seek to annex the global into their own practices of the modern."[22] The imagination is vital and alive, Appadurai says, "a staging ground for action."[23] And he emphasizes that this view of the imagination must be different from Anderson's. It is "explicitly transnational—even postnational."[24]

For Manfred Steger, the stirring of the "postnational imagination" is *The Rise of the Global Imaginary*, the felicitous title of his book.[25] Like Appadurai, Steger recognizes how images, people, and material now circulate more freely across national boundaries, creating a "new sense of 'the global.'"[26] He says "globalization was never merely a matter of increasing flows of capital and goods across national boundaries. Rather, it constitutes a multidimensional set of processes in which images, sound bites, metaphors, myths, symbols and spatial arrangements of globality were just as important as economic and technological dynamics."[27]

Steger emphasizes the importance of the awareness and apprehension of this new globality. The result is an "intensifying 'subjective' recognition of a shrinking world."[28] Steger sees the resulting imaginary as "no longer exclusively articulations of the national imaginary." Indeed, as the national increasingly gives way to the global, the result is a "dawning global imaginary."[29] To return to Anderson's terms, the imagined community is now the globe.

GLOBAL IMAGINARY TO GLOBAL VILLAGE

A global imaginary sounds like a twenty-first-century idea, but as you know, Marshall McLuhan prefigured the concept as early as the 1960s with his notion of the global village. McLuhan was a determinedly controversial personality. His work on media spanned four decades, from the 1950s to his death in 1980, but he rose to prominence in the 1960s and 1970s, during the height of television's popularity and the dawning of computers. He became an international celebrity. He appeared on magazine covers and television talk shows. He portrayed himself in the Woody Allen film *Annie Hall*. *Wired* magazine lists him on its masthead as "patron saint."

In academic circles of the time, however, McLuhan was often a subject of derision and degradation. Perhaps because of his celebrity, his outlandish style, and his broad and sweeping declarations, McLuhan earned the scorn of many scholars. Yet his works continued to be referenced and his ideas debated. As media continued to develop in ways anticipated by his writings, McLuhan edged back into the academy.[30]

Numerous theorists on globalization now cite the value of McLuhan's work. Manuel Castells' title *The Internet Galaxy* pays tribute to *The Gutenberg Galaxy*. Elsewhere, Castells has defended McLuhan. He says, "McLuhan was a genius. The fact that he was not an empirical researcher, but a theorist, has allowed people to think that they can dismiss his insights."[31] Anthony Giddens too has recognized McLuhan's role. Giddens' explorations of how globalization and media transformed space and time derive in part from his study of McLuhan and the Toronto school tradition.[32] And McLuhan's work continues to find traction in studies of globalization and media.[33]

Why do people still find value in McLuhan? In a series of works, *The Mechanical Bride* (1951), *The Gutenberg Galaxy* (1962), *Understanding Media* (1964), and others, McLuhan develops a complex and controversial approach to media. Influenced by his professor and mentor Harold Innis, McLuhan's primary focus is on the transformative effects that electronic media are having on humankind. McLuhan argues that the medium itself is far more important than any content it carries.[34] Indeed, he says, the media physically affect the human central nervous system. They influence the way the brain works and how it processes information. They create new patterns of thought and behavior. For example, he argues that people and societies of the printing press era were shaped by that medium. And people and societies are being shaped in new ways by electronic media. In one of his well-known, provocative dictums, he says, "The medium is the message."[35]

In a related theme, McLuhan also argues that electronic media are "abolishing" space and time.[36] What does he mean? He says humans around the world can see one another and speak with one another as if they are in the same space at the same time—space and time no longer separate people. From that basis, he develops perhaps his most important concept. With the world "made smaller" by electronic media and free from the restrictions of space and time, he says, "the human family now exists under conditions of a 'global village.'" It is a striking metaphor. "The new electronic interdependence recreates the world in the image of a global village."[37]

McLuhan's son Eric believes the term derived from James Joyce's *Finnegans Wake* or Wyndham Lewis' *America and Cosmic Man*, which has the line, "The earth has become one big village, with telephones laid on from one end to the other, and air transport, both speedy and safe."[38] Regardless of its origins, the phrase now regularly appears in common and academic use. "Global Village" is the name of an entertainment and shopping venue in Dubailand, a Habitat for Humanity project, a summer program for young entrepreneurs, a worldwide phone service, and countless other entities. A Google search finds 34.8 million links. To recall McLuhan's original argument in such a context is daunting. Yet serious reflection on the global village may offer ways of apprehending the present and future shape of a rising global imaginary being shaped by globalization and media.

REGAINING BABEL

As I noted in the first chapter, McLuhan places the global village within the Judeo-Christian metaphor of Babel. In the story of Babel, you recall, vain humans try to erect a monument to themselves. But the Lord confounds their language so that they no longer can understand one another. And humanity becomes divided and scattered across the globe. The site of ruin, where humanity was once united in common language, is to be known as Babel.

For McLuhan, media allowed humans to recover the unity they lost at Babel. With humans sharing television images, photographs, films, advertising, video, and more, and with computers providing instant translation, language is not so divisive. McLuhan was exceedingly optimistic:

> Language as the technology of human extension, whose powers of division and separation we know so well, may have been the "Tower of Babel" by which men sought to scale the highest heavens. Today computers hold out the promise of a means of instant translation of any code or language into any other code or language. The computer, in short, promises by technology a Pentecostal condition of universal understanding and unity.[39]

The utopian vision—"a Pentecostal condition of universal understanding and unity"—is striking.[40] McLuhan even imagines the possibility of a kind of collective unconscious, shared by all humans. That is, we would know what each other is thinking and feeling and would exist together in peace. He says,

> The next logical step would seem to be, not to translate, but to by-pass languages in favor of a general cosmic consciousness, which might be very like the collective unconscious dreamt of by Bergson. The condition of "weightlessness," that biologists say promises a physical immortality, may be paralleled by the conditions of speechlessness that could confer a perpetuity of collective harmony and peace.[41]

THE TECHNOLOGICAL SUBLIME

McLuhan eventually backed away from this gloried vision of the future. Writings that appeared after his death underscore his concern about the effect of global media on humankind.[42] However, *Understanding Media* remains McLuhan's most influential work, and its impact continues to be felt. McLuhan had bequeathed to the world a provocative metaphor. The overall global imaginary anticipated by McLuhan is one in which people, through new media, recognize and reclaim their common humanity in a world that evolves into paradisal harmony and peace. The imaginary resonates with lofty visions, idealistic hopes in humanity, and fervent confidence in the power of media technology.

It seems overblown, perhaps, but McLuhan had simply placed himself in a long line of writers and public figures who celebrate and anticipate the role of technology, particularly communication technology, in human life. For example, with language that intriguingly anticipates a global village, Samuel Morse told Congress that his telegraph could "diffuse, with the speed of thought, a knowledge of all that is occurring throughout the land; making, in fact, one neighborhood of the whole country."[43] And it is good to recall that the completion of the first transatlantic telegraph cable in 1858 was greeted by celebrations, bonfires, fireworks, and pageants on both sides of the Atlantic. New York City hosted a mammoth parade, called the largest ever to that point. Just for the telegraph.[44]

Each new technological advance—the telegraph, telephone, film, radio, television, satellite, computer, Internet, cell phone—seems to inspire these redemptive dreams of community and peace. The many books that chronicled the rise of globalization near the turn of the century credited and celebrated media technology, especially digital media, and can be understood in this tradition. Thomas Friedman, in *The Lexus and the Olive Tree*, glowingly defines globalization as "the inexorable integration of markets, nation-states and technologies to a degree never witnessed before—in a way that is enabling individuals, corporations, and nation-states to reach around the world farther, faster, deeper and cheaper than ever before."[45] Recall, too, his hearty embrace of technology in *The World Is Flat*: "*I am a technological determinist! Guilty as charged.*"[46] Another writer of the same period similarly heralds opportunities in a "borderless world" in which business is "carried out through a network of offices and entrepreneurial individuals, connected to each other by crisscrossing lines of communication rather than lines of authority."[47] As Bill Gates, founder of Microsoft, said in an interview, "Never before in history has innovation offered promise of so much to so many in so short a time."[48]

Long ago, Leo Marx, a historian of technology, identified such representations as "the rhetoric of the technological sublime"—treatises that look to technology to bring about a renewed sense of community, equality, humane labor, peace across borders, and other aspirations.[49] Media scholars

James Carey and John J. Quirk, with a nod to Marx, updated the phrase in the 1970s, with the ascension of television and the Internet, as "the rhetoric of the electrical sublime."[50]

From its first appearance in *The Gutenberg Galaxy*, even as the words entered common parlance, the "global village" has often been summarily dispatched as more rhetoric of the technological and the electrical sublime. The cozy concept of the village and the transcendental characterization of its contours have been criticized and satirized in the academic and popular press, and indeed the debate over the concept continues to this day.[51]

LEWIS MUMFORD

However, as we have seen, the global village is still a powerful metaphor. Dismissing the metaphor does not make it go away. Much more interesting and important, especially for a study of globalization and media, is the analysis and censure leveled by Lewis Mumford, another historian of science and technology. Mumford was writing in the same era as McLuhan. Rather than simply deriding and dismissing the metaphor of the global village or its utopian dimensions, Mumford took the metaphor seriously. He laid out the implications of the global village. Mumford's vision can be understood as an alternate global imaginary, an imaginary that may offer insights into the shape of globalization and media in our time—which is not quite seeing cosmic, collective harmony and peace.

THE PENTAGON OF POWER

Mumford was a writer of enormous breadth, producing work on urban issues, architecture, literature, technology, and science. Born in 1895, Mumford lived and chronicled the technological advances of the twentieth century. Like others, he first marveled at the tremendous advances in media technology of the time—film, radio, telephone, and television. In his early writings on media technology and society, Mumford evokes the technological sublime in language that might have guided McLuhan toward the global village. With the development of "the telephone and radio and ultimately television," Mumford writes, "all the inhabitants of the planet could theoretically be linked together for instantaneous communications as closely as the inhabitants of a village."[52]

McLuhan was deeply and admittedly affected by Mumford's early work and cites him throughout his books. James Carey has provided an insightful analysis that demonstrates the influence of Mumford on many of McLuhan's most important ideas, from media as extensions of man, to the abolishment of time and space, to the effect of media on human senses, to the global village.[53] McLuhan greatly appreciated the power of Mumford's insights.

However, the appreciation was not returned. Mumford had watched with ever-deepening dismay as media technology was used not for the betterment of humankind but the betterment of corporations and the military. Rather than peace and prosperity, technology was being used in pursuit of profit and power. Mumford's original fervor for media technology helped fuel a palpable rage over the betrayal. He excoriated what he termed "the pentagon of power"—political absolutism, property, productivity, profit, and publicity.[54] You can almost hear him sputtering the words. And as McLuhan seemed to legitimize and even celebrate the exploitation of media technology by those at the nexus of the pentagon, Mumford turned his considerable talents and scorn on him.

Mumford was enraged, in particular, that McLuhan's elevation of electronic media could lead to the repudiation of the written word. He depicts a resulting, grotesque world of disorder, ignorance, and entropy, "expressed with psychedelic extravagance by Professor Marshall McLuhan and his followers."[55] Ouch. The criticism gets worse. Mumford says, "McLuhan's trancelike vaticinations" offer a world of instantaneous planetary communication in which "mankind as a whole will return to the pre-primitive level, sharing mindless sensations and pre-linguistic communion." Mumford goes on to paint McLuhan's celebration of electronic media as a "burning of the books," such as "the public bonfires lighted by the Nazis."[56] He writes,

> But it remained for McLuhan to picture as technology's ultimate gift a more absolute mode of control: one that will achieve total illiteracy, with no permanent record except that officially committed to the computer, and open only to those permitted access to this facility. This repudiation of an independent written and printed record means nothing less than the erasure of man's diffused, multi-brained collective memory.[57]

Mumford sees special danger in McLuhan's conception of the global village. For Mumford, a global village would be "total cultural dissolution."[58] He acknowledges that electronic communication has "added a new dimension to human capability and practical cooperation." But, he says, "immediate intercourse on a worldwide basis does not necessarily mean a less trivial or parochial personality." In fact, Mumford says, "The lifting of restrictions upon close human intercourse" has been dangerous and increased the areas of friction and mobilized warlike mass reactions.[59]

He looks back over the history of media technology and transportation and notes that the introduction of each technology was accompanied by hopes of worldwide solidarity and political unity. "In the course of two centuries," he says, "these hopes have been discredited. As the technical gains have been consolidated, moral disruptions, antagonisms, and collective massacres have become more flagrant, not in local conflicts alone but on a global scale."[60] His blunt conclusion: "Audio-visual tribalism (McLuhan's 'global village') is a humbug," an "electronic illusion" that would lead to wars, massacres, excommunication of cultures, authoritarian control, subjugation of large populations by the military and corporate elite, and worldwide division—"the electronic Tower of Babel."[61] Mumford thus completes his excoriation by turning back upon McLuhan the beloved metaphor of Babel.

CONCLUSION: A GLOBAL VILLAGE OF BABEL

As you can see, the stakes can be high and the game can be rough in academic theorizing over a global imaginary. What can we conclude? First, the individual and social imaginaries described by Lacan, Castoriadis, Anderson, and Taylor surely are being augmented with increased awareness of globality. As Appadurai and Steger suggest, the economic, cultural, and political processes of globalization in our time have combined with continued advances in media technology to produce a rising global imaginary. The deep divide between Mumford and McLuhan can be understood in this context. Each writer offers a starkly different vision of the results of our global imaginary. Whose vision best aids our understanding of the globe today? Close to fifty years later, we can declare: They both were right.

McLuhan was right. Our era of globalization has seen the realization of the global village. A dawning global imaginary has been made possible in which people can and do imagine themselves as sharing life on the planet in the same way that people long ago understood themselves as sharing life in the village. Travel from one end to the other is not difficult. News and communication are instantaneous. People share stories, songs, videos, images, myths, and more. They are dependent upon one another for resources, goods, and trading, and they compete in those areas as well. The "global village" has

entered common parlance because it captures for many people their conception of the world today—the globe as imagined community.

Globalization and media have indeed partnered over time and, in our
time, created the conditions by which the globe can be imagined as a village. However, this global village is no utopia or paradise, as McLuhan first
prophesied. Nor does the global village suggest a "flat world" or a "borderless world" with access and opportunity for all. Mumford's ferocious
critique has proved true. It does not ultimately deny our now emerging
global village. It shreds McLuhan's transcendental depiction of life in that
village. Rather than the restoration of unity before Babel that McLuhan
foresaw, the dawning global imaginary offers a village dominated by corporate and military elites, a village characterized not by understanding, unity,
or community, but a village torn by contest, control, suffering, struggle, and
separation—a return to Babel.

As Mumford warned, more contact does not mean more peace, more
communication does not mean more community, and more trade does not
mean more cooperation. Power and profit, themes that haunt Mumford's
work but play little part in McLuhan's, have confounded humankind again.
Unlike Innis, his mentor, McLuhan paid little heed to economics, power,
politics, and the likely collision of global and local cultures. He did not at
first apprehend how these forces would polarize life in the global village,
dividing it into a Babel of contesting languages, opposing ideologies and
beliefs, and savage struggles for resources and power.

As I was preparing this book for publication, I came across a passage
from Arjun Appadurai, who also sought to capture the dystopian potential
of the global village. Appadurai says,

> We are now aware that with media, each time we are tempted to speak
> of the global village, we must be reminded that media create communi-
> ties with "no sense of place." The world we live in now seems rhizomic,
> even schizophrenic, calling for theories of rootlessness, alienation, and
> psychological distance between individuals and groups on the one hand,
> and fantasies (or nightmares) of electronic propinquity on the other.[62]

With tens of thousands of the globe's children dying each day from
starvation and disease, with one billion people living in desperate poverty,
with contemplation and reflection throttled by incessant and omnipresent
media, with holy lands cleaved by hatred, with families torn asunder, with
giant slums growing each day outside the world's biggest cities, with violence and terror haunting terminals and stations, a global village of "universal understanding and unity" seems a pathetic and preposterous absurdity.

McLuhan himself, seemingly from the grave, came to endorse a quite darker vision of the global village. *The Global Village: Transformations in World Life and Media in the 21st Century* was published almost ten years after McLuhan's death, cowritten by McLuhan and Bruce Powers. The authors appear eager to disavow the transcendental enthusiasm of McLuhan's more celebrated work. They describe a world of "massive unemployment in the industrial nations, a destruction of all privacy, and a planetary disequilibrium keyed to continent-wide propaganda skirmishes conducted through the new-found utility of interactive satellites."[63] They also see a future of cable channels divided by culture and language, banks retooled for money handling to different cultures, neighborhood schools each with a diverse language, and ethnicities congregated in self-integrated barrios. Cities will harbor "a gestaltic political conglomeration of whites, blacks, Asians, and Hispanics fighting with each other for what is left of the economic pie in a nation of a declining birthrate of native-born Americans and an aging white population."[64] They see "centers everywhere and margins nowhere in a new tribalism."[65] And finally, one possible result of "global media networking," they suggest in a cryptic warning, is that it "brings back Tower of Babel."[66] Cosmic, collective harmony has been throttled before birth.

Aided, then, by the insights of both Mumford and McLuhan, the contours of our world come into view. We are being drawn closer and closer together, but that closeness is yielding friction and division. The historical, ongoing but erratic economic, cultural, and political processes of globalization, combined with electronic and digital media, pulled and twisted by humankind's hubris, vanity, and greed, are yielding a cheerless, bleak perspective of an emerging world, a global village of Babel.

Are we sentenced to live in that world? As we have repeated throughout, globalization and media result from the actions of people, and those actions can be halted or altered. Though the "pentagon of power" is firmly entrenched, change is not impossible. A place to begin is understanding how the economic, political, and cultural processes of globalization join with media to create our global village, and so the next chapter takes up profit and penury—economic globalization and media in the global village.

5

MEDIA AND ECONOMIC GLOBALIZATION

Starving Children, *Hannah Montana*, Football, and the Bottom Billion

NESTLÉ, MARKETING, AND AN INFANT FORMULA CONTROVERSY

Suppose you are a young woman in Africa who has just given birth to a son. You know that infants die often in your land. Infant mortality rates in some African countries are near 25 percent. One in every four babies will die before they reach their first birthday. They die mostly from diseases such as cholera and malaria. The diseases take a terrible toll. They wrack the baby with fever. They dehydrate the baby through diarrhea and vomiting. You are deathly afraid your new baby may die.

You see a pamphlet from Nestlé, a well-known company that for more than a century has been making infant formula—the liquid food product used as a substitute for breast feeding. The pamphlet says the formula is "the new 'Gold Standard' in infant nutrition." It says the product "protects" babies and "prevents diarrhea." Would you use the product or breast feed?

The truth is that breast feeding is by far the safest, most nutritious, and of course cheapest way to feed a baby. So why would the executive board and board of directors of Nestlé allow the company to advertise its product in this land and in this way? More than 1.5 million babies die each year because they are not adequately breast fed. The United Nations Children's Fund (UNICEF) estimates that a non-breast-fed child in developing countries with irregular electricity and unhygienic conditions can be twenty-five times more likely to die of diarrhea and four times more likely to die of pneumonia than a breast-fed child.[1]

Infant formula, in fact, can be a disaster in developing countries. Formula is often mixed with water, which can be contaminated in poor lands. Because of lack of education, many women also do not know they must sterilize baby bottles after every feeding. Even if they do know, many mothers do not always have the necessary electricity or fuel to boil water regularly. Many of the mothers are poor. They try to be frugal and use less formula than the directions state in order to make the formula last longer, but the babies then get less nutrition.

On the other hand, nature provided humans with breast milk so they would survive and thrive in the crucial first months of life. Breast milk is plentiful, healthy, and free. Breast milk has natural nutrients and antibodies that formula lacks. Breast milk protects babies, better than formula, from diarrhea, bacterial meningitis, respiratory infections, and other diseases.

So the question again: Why would Nestlé officials advertise their product in this land and in this way? The answer: money.

Many of us know Nestlé as the maker of chocolate, Toll House cookies, and hot cocoa. However, Nestlé is the number-one producer of infant formula in the world. For more than twenty years, advocacy groups and nongovernmental organizations (NGOs) have accused Nestlé of unethical practices in promoting infant formula over breast milk in developing countries. In countries around the world, Nestlé is in fact the number-one boycotted product. UNICEF, while not commenting directly on Nestlé, has said, "Marketing practices that undermine breastfeeding are potentially hazardous wherever they are pursued: in the developing world, WHO estimates that some 1.5 million children die each year because they are not adequately breastfed. These facts are not in dispute."[2]

"Attention Must Be Paid"

We will look more closely at Nestlé and its marketing practices in this chapter. We have been building a case that media and globalization have been essential partners in human history and that together they have built, thus far, a global village of Babel, a world of inequality and division. To understand all this, we have emphasized human action throughout. And we have suggested that the vague concept of globalization is best studied by breaking it down into three processes—economic, political, and cultural. This chapter explores media and economic globalization.

Often, my students in global studies—who are interested in culture, music, sports, religion, identity, migration, and other aspects of media and globalization—protest that they do not want to talk about economics or markets or capitalism. It's *business* and it's boring, they say. But as soon as we talk in concrete terms about human beings and human actions—Should Nestlé officials market infant formula in developing countries? Should six companies own most of the world's media? Should *Hannah Montana* have even existed?—well, then the conversations are hard to stop. Media and economic globalization can offer intriguing and important issues to consider.

This chapter makes three points about the essential ties between media and economic globalization in the construction of our world. First, the chapter will argue that the media make economic globalization possible by creating the conditions for global capitalism and by promoting the conceptual foundation of the world's market economy. Economic globalization, we see again, is story and myth—narratives that make natural the buying and selling of products across borders and boundaries and mythic celebrations of products and consumption. Advertising—the primary support of media in our times—is the main vehicle for such celebrations, celebrations that go on even in the face of vast inequalities and even when products and practices may lead to the deaths of infants.

Second, yet of crucial importance, the media are themselves now huge transnational global corporations that help drive globalization even as they embody globalization. Newspapers, magazines, and radio and television stations were not long ago primarily local media, owned by local people, serving regional and only sometimes national audiences. Media now are the epitome of economic globalization. Much of the world's media is owned or controlled by a handful of conglomerates that span the globe in pursuit of markets and profits.

The chapter next will go more deeply into the relationship of media and economic globalization. I will point out how the media have been essential conduits for worldwide business information, communication, and transactions. I ask if modern-day capitalism would even be possible without media. I then heed Roland Barthes' wise observation that what goes unsaid by myths is as important as what gets said. And modern myths of economic globalization leave much unsaid. Media are filled with stories of CEOs, corporations, and every vibration of the stock market. However, despite the proliferation and expansion of media, the world's most pressing issues and problems receive scant attention. A billion people—the "bottom billion"—still live in terrible poverty, many of them now in sprawling slums on the margins of megacities.[3] To take a line from a play, "Attention must be paid" to these bottom billion, not only for their sake but the sake of the world.[4] Finally, we will focus on a lone journalist who indeed tried to tell the story of the bottom billion.

HOW TO SELL SHOES: FROM COBBLERS TO NIKE

Let's start with a simple pair of shoes. For centuries, if people wanted shoes, they made them themselves or they knew a nearby shoemaker, or cobbler, who cobbled the shoes together from tanned leather and string. If people were traveling, information on shoes for sale or barter might be written on papyrus or parchment and posted at trading sites—the first advertisements. More permanent traders might paint on a rock or wall—the first billboards. As people moved to villages, towns, and cities, however, they might not know where to find the cobbler. Most people were unable to read, so the cobbler would hang a sign with a picture of a shoe or boot outside his shop. The sign would compete for attention on the street with signs for hats, watches, horseshoes, and perhaps even another shoemaker.

The printing press added another dimension to the advertising of shoes. More people became literate. Handbills and pamphlets could be given out announcing shoemaking locations and services. In the seventeenth century, printed advertisements started to appear in newspapers and magazines. People could compare advertisements before buying shoes. Competition changed the nature of the advertisement. Cobblers now not only had to publicize their location, but they also needed to compete with other cobblers. How would they do that? They might state that they had lower prices or special materials or unique fashions.[5]

Eventually cobblers banded together to make shoes more efficiently. These groups eventually became factories, and competition grew fiercer. Advertising was created not only to announce locations and products, but to convince consumers to buy a particular brand of shoes. Shoemakers developed increasingly sophisticated messages to persuade people to purchase their products. As each new communication medium was introduced—from film to radio to television to the Internet—shoemakers used those media to market their products. And then came Nike.

MEDIA, MARKETING, AND MYTH: "JUST DO IT"

I wish I could insert one of the classic Nike television commercials here or display Nike's interactive Web page or numerous Facebook sites. In our time, Nike is one of the world's largest shoemakers—we can't quite call them cobblers anymore. The company epitomizes the marriage of media, marketing, and economic globalization. It was founded in 1964 as Blue Ribbon Sports by a University of Oregon track athlete, Philip Knight, and his coach, Bill Bowerman. Under Knight's direction, the company became Nike—named after the Greek goddess of victory—in 1978 and now sells sportswear and equipment worldwide, with revenues of close to $20 billion a year.[6]

Advertising is a primary reason. Nike used its distinct logo (the swoosh) and slogans ("Just Do It") to establish itself as a premium brand. People pay close to two hundred dollars for a pair of shoes that costs less than ten dollars to produce. Why do people do that? Nike advertising associates Nike products with superior qualities, such as hard work, initiative, and success. Advertising associates Nike products with superior athletes, such as Michael Jordan, Tiger Woods, Maria Sharapova, and Serena Williams. In this way, advertising offers us modern-day myths. Stories of exemplary figures—heroes—struggling and succeeding through adversity are at the heart of myth. Nike advertising—and much advertising in general—links these modern-day heroes to products. The advertisements suggest that to link ourselves to those heroes or heroic qualities, we simply need to purchase the product. It turns out that people will pay a lot of money to be associated with superior qualities, even if that association is on their feet.

The idea works, and it works worldwide. After succeeding in the United States, Nike applied similar tactics in other lands and found similar success. Visit the Nike website today and you will be greeted with a menu from which you must choose among fourteen different languages. Nike makes shoes in few of those countries. But it advertises and sells—and sells a lot—in all of them.[7]

We are at the heart of economic globalization, which has opened up markets worldwide. It is important to emphasize the crucial role of the media in economic globalization. The media foster the conditions for global capitalism. They fill our days with invitations and exhortations for consumption, from ceaseless commercials on radio and television, to product placement in films, to digital billboards, to pop-up ads, to broadsheets in bathroom stalls. The media fill these channels with mythic celebrations of consumers, products, and markets. These myths are most readily seen in advertising and marketing, which drive consumption and expansion in the global village. But many media stories—in newspapers, magazines, television, and film—also celebrate global capitalism.

Yet the celebration is not shared by all. Indeed, advertising, especially as it crosses borders, often comes under harsh scrutiny and criticism. Nike's success, for example, has not come without controversy. China banned a Nike ad that shows basketball start LeBron James defeating Chinese characters, including kung fu masters, two Chinese women in traditional dress, and dragons. For years, Nike has had to fight a public relations battle against accusations of running "sweatshops"—overseas factories where workers are overworked and underpaid to make Nike shoes.[8] The company has been sued for wrongfully using the Beatles' song "Revolution" in its advertising. The company has been criticized for running advertising campaigns for products in areas where people cannot afford them, creating a demand sometimes met by robbery and violence. Reports continue to surface of young people killed for their Nike sneakers.[9] Nike myths must run full time to keep up.[10]

NESTLÉ: JUST DON'T DO IT?

However, perhaps the most famous and long-standing controversy over global marketing is the marketing of infant formula in Africa by the Swiss firm Nestlé. As I noted at the beginning of the chapter, for more than twenty years the company has been accused of unethical practices in promoting infant formula in poor and developing countries. Its marketing campaigns, critics say, have led to death and disease throughout the developing world.[11]

The company's roots date back to 1867, when Swiss pharmacist Henri Nestlé mixed cow's milk, wheat flour, and sugar for a neighbor's baby who would not nurse from the breast. From this beginning, the company first specialized in infant formula and condensed milk before mergers and acquisitions helped it become one of the largest food conglomerates in the world. It sells coffee, cookies, canned and frozen vegetables, and candy as well as L'Oréal cosmetics and Friskies and Alpo pet foods. It remains the world leader in infant formula, with more than 50 percent of the market.

The storm over Nestlé's marketing practices began in the 1960s. Birth rates in developed countries were starting to level off. Infant formula producers looked for new markets in less-developed nations. Those countries had little history or experience with infant formula. Marketing and advertising were needed to promote the product. Some NGOs, such as Save the Children, began to accuse Nestlé of unethical promotions.[12] The International Baby Food Action Network (IBFAN) and Baby Milk Action claimed that Nestlé distributed free powdered formula samples to women in hospitals and maternity wards.[13] When women use the formula and do not breast feed, the breast eventually no longer produces milk. When the free formula runs out, the women must continue to buy the formula to feed their babies. The groups claimed that the company dressed people to look like nurses or health care workers to distribute the formula. They said the company offered gifts to persuade hospital workers to promote and distribute its formula.[14]

Nestlé denied all the charges, but in 1977, a remarkable global boycott was begun against the company. Pressure and publicity from the boycott helped lead the World Health Organization and UNICEF to develop international codes for the marketing of infant formula. Nestlé agreed to the code, and the boycott appeared over.[15] However, almost immediately, NGOs again charged that Nestlé and others were ignoring the code.[16] In 1999, Britain's Advertising Standards Authority found that Nestlé's claims to have acted "ethically and responsibly" could not be supported; in 2000, the European Parliament also pursued allegations against the company.[17]

The boycott and monitoring of Nestlé continue, primarily coordinated by the British group Baby Milk Action and IBFAN, which now have a presence in more than one hundred countries. Nestlé continues to deny charges,[18] but as I write, the Nestlé website advertises its latest formula as the "Gold Standard" in infant nutrition.[19]

It is not often that media and marketing are charged with causing the deaths of children. However, the controversy surrounding Nestlé symbolizes the sometimes troubling impact of global corporations and marketing practices on peoples and cultures. More broadly, the controversy simply serves as a reminder of the omnipresent influence of marketing in economic globalization. As media scholar Robert McChesney reminds us, "Economic and cultural globalization arguably would be impossible without a global commercial media system to promote global markets and to encourage consumer values."[20] McChesney and coauthor Edward Herman call global media "the new missionaries of global capitalism."[21]

MEDIA OLIGOPOLY

An especially important economic fact when considering media and globalization is an especially ugly word: *oligopoly*. It sounds like some ancient monster, doesn't it? *Oligopoly* has connections to the more common word *monopoly*, which is when a single company controls all of a product or service. If everyone in the United States could get telephone service from only one company, such as AT&T, then AT&T would have a monopoly. For most of the 1900s, AT&T indeed had a legal monopoly over U.S. telephones and telephone service. An oligopoly is when a few companies control a product or service.

Why talk of media and oligopoly? The world seems saturated with different media. It's hard to believe that the media—the world's media—are controlled by just a few companies. As a journalism professor, for example, I use many, varied media each day. When I am in New York, maybe the media capital of the world, I have hundreds of choices. I might start the day waking to music and news on radio station WPLJ, then turn on the television to watch *Good Morning America* and get local weather from WABC-TV before turning to ESPN for sports news. On my way to meetings, I might listen to music by Breaking Benjamin or other artists. During the day, in between talks, I might read magazines like *Discover* or read books like *The Last Lecture* by Professor Randy Pausch. Back home, I will try to catch *World News with Diane Sawyer* and then perhaps watch the end of *Grey's Anatomy* before turning on football or a movie, such as one of the *Pirates of the Caribbean* series with Johnny Depp. That seems like a lot of different media from a lot of different companies. But, as you might have guessed, all those different media companies—WPLJ, *Good Morning America*, WABC-TV, ESPN, Buena Vista Music, *Discover* magazine, Hyperion Books, the ABC network, and Touchstone Pictures—are owned by one big conglomerate: the Walt Disney Company.

Around the world, once small, local, and regional media companies—newspapers, magazines, radio stations, television and cable channels, book publishers, movie studios, Internet sites, and more—are being bought up by a handful of huge global conglomerates and corporations, who themselves were once small and local. It has all happened incredibly fast, primarily in the last twenty-five years. The result goes by various names—media oligopoly, consolidation, concentration, and convergence. By some estimates, six companies—in particular, Disney, Time Warner, News Corporation, Viacom, Vivendi, and Bertelsmann—own or control close to 75 percent of the world's media.[22]

Many of my students are surprised and dismayed to learn of these conglomerates. Others, though, shrug their shoulders. They ask if such development isn't natural or the result of successful business decisions. I have to show them that the growth of these media conglomerates is not some natural law of nature, in which the strong survive and get bigger. In fact, to become conglomerates, companies must hammer away at local, state, and national governments. They work continually behind the scenes. They lobby, market, and persuade. And, ultimately, they get handsome favors and concessions from officials and lawmakers.

McChesney has extensively studied the global media oligopoly. He argues that a host of political decisions, including deregulation, support for market expansion, government intervention, and more, have paved the way for conglomerates to expand worldwide. He writes,

> The global media system is not the result of "free markets" or natural law; it is the consequence of a number of important state policies that have been made that created the system. The media giants have had a heavy hand in drafting these laws and regulations, and the public tends to have little or no input. In the United States, the corporate media lobbies are notorious for their ability to get their way with politicians, especially if their adversary is not another powerful corporate sector, but that amorphous entity called the "public interest."[23]

IMPLICATIONS OF MEDIA OLIGOPOLY: IS BIG BAD?

My students also ask: Is big bad? The media oligopoly is more than just an interesting and important fact of modern life. It has numerous implications for economics, politics, and culture. The global oligopoly, it must be said, is not all bad. It is superb at producing commercial, escapist entertainment enjoyed around the world. And in some countries, especially those under authoritarian control, some themes in that entertainment, such as the independence of women or importance of education, might resonate with political or cultural meaning. Yet many scholars and policy makers worry deeply about the repercussions of the world's media being in the hands of a half dozen conglomerates. What are the issues?

A first concern is that the media oligopoly is primarily owned and controlled by Western companies, mostly headquartered in the United States. Decision making over content, distribution, investment, and expansion is made far away from the local cultures that will be affected by those decisions. Investments or programming that might be needed at the local level will be unknown—foreign—to the executives nestled in Manhattan offices.

Thus, a related concern: Sometimes the conglomerates print or broadcast content unwanted by those trying to uphold local customs. Films involving gory violence, drug use, and other topics can go against cultural traditions. Such content sometimes leads to local protests and prohibitions. The violent series of films *Saw* and *Halloween* have been banned in Malaysia.[24] The sexually provocative fare of some shows on MTV International has caused consternation in numerous nations. Katy Perry's hit single "I Kissed a Girl" was removed from airplay in Dubai.[25] Sexual and political content also causes local tensions. *Brokeback Mountain* was banned in China and other nations for its depiction of homosexuality.[26] The hit video game *Call of Duty: Modern Warfare II* was almost banned in Russia because Russians appear as terrorists in the game.[27] Nations and cultures resent having such media introduced into their lands by companies looking to sell products.

Local cultures, however, can offer few alternatives. Most simply do not have the resources to regularly produce products that can compete against the giants of oligopoly. For example, Hollywood production companies can bankroll multimillion-dollar films with the world's most popular actors and actresses. One Hollywood film can cost more than entire nations spend on film production in a year. And Western conglomerates can market and support their efforts with the many different platforms they control. Small local film and music producers find themselves having to compete, often unsuccessfully, against transnational giants who control local airwaves, advertising, theaters, television stations, and more.

Entire traditions of filmmaking and music are at stake in some locales. Countries must fight hard, sometimes with quotas against the conglomerates and subsidies for the small artists, to preserve and protect their cultures. The European Union has a quota that assures that 50 percent of television programming is produced in the EU (not, by contrast, in the United States). Numerous smaller nations, such as Norway, Denmark, and Spain, provide support for their culture industries. Italy gives subsidies to its struggling film companies, which strive to keep alive the long Italian tradition of filmmakers that includes Federico Fellini, Roberto Rossellini, and Bernardo Bertolucci.[28]

A widespread concern in many lands over the media conglomerates is captured in the term *cultural imperialism* or *electronic colonialism*. The worry is that Western culture, especially American culture, will be *imposed* on other countries by the oppressive omnipresence of Western cultural products in their lands. As media scholar Thomas McPhail argues, "All of the US multimedia empires, along with their extensive advertising networks, project and encourage US tastes, values, mores, history, culture, and language around the world."[29] The huge reach of the conglomerates allows them to market Western music, food, fashion, appliances, cars and every other item, swamping the ability of local cultures to offer alternatives.

However, others contend that local cultures are resilient and strong, and that local people continue to show appreciation for content with their own language, culture, and tradition. People pick and choose among local and global offerings, sometimes combining them in imaginative ways.[30] We will look more deeply into this question in our chapter on cultural globalization. But the issue is very much a part of debates over media and economic globalization.

"GLOBAL VILLAGE OR GLOBAL PILLAGE"?

McChesney has developed a nuanced view of the implications of economic globalization and media. He contends that the media oligopoly is not interested in the ideology of the global village or the evangelizing of cultural values. The oligopoly is interested in one thing: profit.

"The global media system," McChesney says, "is better understood, then, as one that advances corporate and commercial interests and values, and denigrates or ignores that which cannot be incorporated into its mission."[31] He continues, "The logical consequence of a commercial media system is less to instill adherence to any ruling powers that be—though that can and does of course happen—than to promote a general belief that politics is unimportant and that there is little hope for organized social change."[32]

In her study of the European Union, Katharine Sarikakis found a similar dynamic. She says that "the normative framework, necessary for the legitimization of policies that transformed the media across Europe, redefined the public in its relation to the media, as consumers of media services and accumulators of cultural goods, rather than as members of an informed and active citizenry."[33] Similarly, critical theorists, such as Adorno and Horkheimer, argued long ago that a "culture industry," which produced mindless entertainment, had great social, political, and economic importance.[34] Such entertainment, they said, can distract audiences from critical thinking, sapping time and energy from social and political action.

Transnational conglomerates, in this view, are much less interested than local media outlets in providing news and information necessary for citizens. People are encouraged to think of products not politics. They are consumers, not citizens. The conglomerates have little incentive to invest in local talk shows, news channels, documentaries, or other social and political content. The global oligopoly of media thus helps create a passive apolitical populace that rises from the couch primarily for consumption.

You likely won't hear about that on the Fox Network or the Disney Channel. Another, perhaps unsurprising, facet of the media oligopoly is the lack of reporting on oligopolies and their effects on the world. The media certainly are not the only business that has seen conglomeration. Some of the world's most vital industries—from petroleum to automobile manufacturing to banking—are controlled by oligopolies. We have already seen that a primary goal for oligopolies is profit making. In a global economy, that means corporations seek around the world for the least expensive location to produce goods. Nations and communities, competing to attract such investments, try to reduce the cost of doing business. In some cases, they reduce labor costs, thus lowering wages for workers. They reduce environmental costs, thus allowing pollution and degradation of the land and skies. They reduce social costs, thus cutting back on social services. These actions have enormous implications.

In a provocatively titled book, *Global Village or Global Pillage*, Jeremy Brecher and Tim Costello decry this "race to the bottom." They say

> All over the world, people are being pitted against each other to see who will offer global corporations the lowest labor, social, and environmental costs. Their jobs are being moved to places with inferior wages, lower business taxes, and more freedom to pollute. Their employers are using the threat of "foreign competition" to hold down wages, salaries, taxes, and environmental protections and to replace high-quality jobs with temporary, part-time, insecure, and low-quality jobs. Their government officials are justifying cuts in education, health, and other services as necessary to reduce business taxes in order to keep or attract jobs.[35]

Mary Robinson has been a tireless advocate for connecting social justice to economic globalization. The first woman president of Ireland and a former United Nations high commissioner for human rights, Robinson founded Realizing Rights: The Ethical Globalization Initiative. She wryly told a 2009 UN session of delegates, NGOs, and others, "People laughed at first when I brought together those two words—ethical globalization." Yet, Robinson said, social justice must be at the root of a fair globalization. And, she said pointedly, media must play an important role. "We need to use modern means of communication to concert more together."[36]

I don't think the media need to "take sides" on the subject of oligopolies. I don't think economic globalization in the global village always produces injustice and exploitation. However, the increasing influence of conglomerates on modern life calls for scrutiny. And media oligopolies most often show little interest in serious reflection on the subject of oligopolies.

A CLOSER LOOK: THE WALT DISNEY COMPANY

How extensive is the media oligopoly? I have suggested some of the holdings of Disney. But to give a sense of the vast reach of these conglomerates and why people are so concerned about the implications of oligopoly, I'll provide a brief summary of the wide-reaching ventures of the top three media giants in the global village. I will start with Disney.

In the 1920s, Walt Disney was a struggling cartoonist who was trying to make a living drawing political cartoons and advertisements. With nothing to lose, he tried his hand at a relatively new medium—animated cartoons that could be shown in local movie theaters. Disney found some success and worked in studios in Kansas City, Hollywood, and New York. In the late 1920s, Disney introduced a new character, a talking mouse. Originally named Mortimer, the character finally was named Mickey, and Mickey Mouse went on to become one of the most successful cartoon characters of all time.[37]

Disney was ambitious. Even as he produced short cartoons with Mickey Mouse, he made plans for an animated full-length feature film. Hollywood producers scoffed at the hubris. But *Snow White and the Seven Dwarfs* became the top motion picture of 1938. Disney won an Oscar (and seven miniature Oscar statues for the dwarves). A series of now-classic films followed, including *Pinocchio, Fantasia, Bambi,* and *Dumbo.*

Disney's ambitions were not sated. He wanted next to build a southern California amusement park based on Disney characters. In 1955, Disneyland opened and would become a major tourist attraction. And still Disney continued. He began to produce feature-length films with live actors, such as *Old Yeller, The Shaggy Dog,* and *Pollyanna.* He began a daily television show, *The Mickey Mouse Club,* and then a weekly, *The Wonderful World of Disney.* In the 1960s, Disney began planning an East Coast theme park near Orlando, Florida. In 1966, however, he learned that he had an advanced stage of lung cancer. He died in December 1966.[38]

The Disney empire—now the Walt Disney Company—continued to grow.[39] In 1971, Walt Disney World opened in Orlando. Feature films rolled out regularly. And the company steadily purchased media properties to add to its holdings. Theme parks were opened worldwide. Television and radio stations were bought around the United States. In the mid-1990s, Disney bought one of the big three U.S. networks—Capital Cities/ABC—and got controlling interest in one of cable television's most successful properties: ESPN. The company also purchased interests in a number of high-profile cable television channels, such as A&E and the History Channel. Here is a summary of holdings that Disney owns or in which it has significant interests:

- ABC television, which produces news shows such as *Good Morning America* and entertainment programs such as *Desperate Housewives* and *Modern Family;*
- television production and distribution companies Touchstone and Buena Vista;

- ABC radio networks with more than seventy stations;
- ten other U.S. TV stations and affiliated radio stations in major cities;
- top cable TV channels, including the Disney Channel, ESPN, ESPN2, ESPNews, ESPN International, Lifetime, A&E, E! Entertainment, and the History Channel;
- three major film studios—Miramax, Touchstone, and Walt Disney Pictures—which have produced hits such as *TRON* and *Toy Story*;
- book publishing, including Hyperion Press and Disney Publishing;
- music recording, including the Hollywood, Mammoth, and Walt Disney labels;
- theme parks and resorts, including Disneyland, Disney World, and EuroDisney;
- Club Disney, a restaurant chain;
- the Disney Cruise Line; and
- Disney stores worldwide.[40]

Hannah Montana *and Vertical Integration*

One of the benefits of such vast holdings is what economists call "vertical integration." A perfect example is the Disney phenomenon *Hannah Montana*. In a traditional business model, a company seeks horizontal integration. To expand, the company looks to purchase properties horizontally—on the same plane or one similar to its current business. A growing book dealer, for example, will buy out a smaller book dealer and thus expand horizontally. The model of vertical integration suggests that companies will purchase properties different from—but complementary to—their current business. Those properties will work in "synergy" with each other. The bookseller might buy a chain of coffee shops; the coffee can be sold in the bookstores; the coffee shops can promote the books. Disney takes vertical integration to the extreme. Many, if not all, of its properties, are designed to complement and support others.

Hannah Montana was an American television series about a girl who by day was an average high school student (Miley Stewart, played by Miley Cyrus) and by night a famous pop singer (Hannah Montana). The show debuted in March 2006 on the Disney Channel and also aired on the Disney-owned ABC Kids block. *Hannah Montana* was extremely successful, with high ratings and many award nominations, and ran for almost five years.

Yet the show was more remarkable as a business model. The premise and casting were quite purposeful.[41] By building a show around a pop singer,

Disney had a vehicle that could, first, create a pop star and, second, introduce pop songs and videos that could be produced and supported by other arms of the business company. Almost immediately, songs sung by Hannah Montana on the show by Disney were collected on CDs made by Disney and played on radio stations owned by Disney. At least one CD was produced every year.

The large and perhaps surprising success of *Hannah Montana*, however, soon pointed to other moneymaking opportunities. The show was such a hit with young girls that by December 2006, just in time for holiday shopping, Disney produced a series of *Hannah Montana* products, such as clothing, jewelry, and dolls, to be sold in Disney stores. Disney followed with a movie—a *Hannah Montana* concert film—which the company produced and promoted on its radio, television, and cable stations.

Hannah Montana was becoming such a success that Disney held an "80-person, all-platform international meeting" to discuss other opportunities.[42] The company quickly created a series of CDs and then *Hannah Montana: The Movie* based on the show. The movie was promoted on Disney radio and television stations, including the Disney Channel and ABC. The show continued to gain in popularity. At its height, the audience was two hundred million, in dozens of nations worldwide. The show's final episode was shown in January 2011. The five-year run had earned the company billions.[43] *Hannah Montana*, as an all-platform franchise, had enriched numerous branches of the Walt Disney Company and offered a sterling example of vertical integration and media-fueled economic globalization.

RUPERT MURDOCH, NEWS CORP., FOX, AND FOOTBALL

In 1953, Rupert Murdoch owned one newspaper, the *Adelaide News*, in South Australia. In 2011, he owned more media than perhaps anyone on the planet. With a net worth of close to $7 billion, he is among the wealthiest people in the world and is often listed among the most powerful. His story offers fascinating insights into the construction of a media conglomerate.

Born in Australia, Murdoch took over his father's newspaper at age twenty-two. Even at that age, he understood expansion. He undertook horizontal integration and began buying newspapers throughout Australia. He would eventually own 70 percent of the country's papers.[44] Yet he was only beginning. He made acquisitions in Britain and the United States, buying the *Sun* in London in 1969, the *San Antonio Express-News* in 1973, and the *New York Post* in 1976. Murdoch's vision, though, was grand. In 1985, he bought the Twentieth Century Fox movie studio. He also wanted to get into U.S. television, but law stipulated that only American citizens could own television stations. In 1985, Murdoch became a naturalized U.S. citizen and bought six local television stations. At the time, the United States had just three national television networks with no plans to add another. Murdoch shrewdly worked around the problem by continuing to buy local television stations in large cities. The collection of local stations was then brought together under the new Fox Network.[45]

Despite numerous stations and some hit shows, such as *The Simpsons, Married . . . With Children,* and *Beverly Hills, 90210,* Fox was not considered on par with the big three networks. Murdoch felt that America's top television sport—NFL football—would give the network greater profile and credibility. In 1993, Murdoch made an offer that the NFL could not refuse—$1.58 billion for four years, outbidding the CBS network by $100 million. It was a savvy coup. Fox used the NFL broadcasts to promote its other shows and legitimize itself as a network. Over the four years of its first NFL contract, Fox transformed the big three into the big four.[46]

Murdoch also entered other arenas and nations. He established the Fox News Channel on U.S. cable television. He purchased MySpace to secure an Internet presence. He purchased Star TV of Hong Kong, the largest satellite television network in Asia. He bought Dow Jones, owner of the *Wall Street Journal,* and positioned that paper to compete with the *New York Times.* In every continent, Murdoch has established a media presence. Media observer James Fallows writes,

> Many see him as a power-mad, rapacious right-wing vulgarian. Rupert Murdoch has indeed been relentless in building a one-of-a kind media network that spans the world. What really drives him, though, is not ideology but a cool concern for the bottom line—and the belief that the media should be treated like any other business, not as a semi-sacred public trust. . . . Rupert Murdoch has seen the future, and it is him.[47]

However, in 2011, Murdoch's bottom-line approach to the media may have caused fractures in his empire. One of his profitable British newspapers, *News of the World,* was charged with hacking into the phone of a teenage murder victim and impeding the police investigation into the killing. Soon after these allegations, more possible hacking victims emerged, including other murdered children, 2005 London bombing casualties, the families of dead soldiers, former Prime Minister Gordon Brown, and the victims of the September 11 terrorist attacks.[48] Murdoch's company was investigated in Britain and the United States, and the momentum of his global expansion was stalled. Even still, News Corp. remains a dominant media mogul. A summary of major holdings includes the following:

- the U.S. Fox television network;
- more than twenty other U.S. television stations;
- Fox News Channel;
- cable channels that include FX, Fox Sports Net, the National Geographic Channel, and the Big 10 Network;
- interests in DirectTV;
- STAR television stations throughout Asia;
- Interests in British Sky Broadcasting (BSkyB) satellite TV service, and other Sky TV channels across Europe, such as Sky Deutschland and Sky Italia;
- Twentieth Century Fox film studio, producer of films such as *Black Swan* and *Avatar*;
- Twentieth Television, and other U.S. and international TV producers and distributors;
- Internet properties, such as Hulu.com;
- more than 125 daily newspapers, including *The Times* (of London), the *New York Post*, and the *Wall Street Journal*, as well as 70 percent of Australia's newspaper circulation; and
- book publishers, including HarperCollins.

TIME WARNER: FROM *LIFE* TO CNN TO AOL

Time Warner displays its conglomeration in its name, which is a combination of two media powerhouses—publishing giant Time Inc. and film and broadcast giant Warner Communications. But the name does not adequately convey the multitude of holdings in the company, which includes Turner Broadcasting, CNN, and more.

Henry Luce and partner Briton Hadden founded Time Inc. in 1922 so they could bring to fruition the idea of a weekly newsmagazine—*Time*. First published in 1923, *Time* became a hugely successful enterprise, and Luce built on this success with other titles such as *Fortune*, *Life*, and *Sports Illustrated*.[49] After Luce's death, the company continued to develop successful magazines, such as *People*, *Entertainment Weekly*, and *Marie Claire*.

Warner also has a storied history. The Warner brothers emigrated from Poland in the early 1900s and opened a movie theater in Pennsylvania. The brothers transformed that business into one of Hollywood's most successful studios, with classic films and top actors and actresses such as Al Jolson, James Cagney, Humphrey Bogart, Joan Crawford, and Bette Davis. The brothers understood corporate expansion.[50] They also created a cartoon unit that produced popular figures such as Porky Pig, Daffy Duck, and Bugs Bunny for film and eventually television, and they produced other television shows as well. In addition, Warner Bros. Records produced musical artists such as Frank Sinatra. They brought all this together under a new name, Warner Communications.[51]

In 1989, looking at the growth of media conglomerates around them, Time Inc. and Warner Communications married their two franchises in a colossal merger. The company was now represented across all media platforms and had the resources to grow further. In another startling move, the conglomerate purchased Turner Broadcasting System, which added CNN, the Cartoon Network, and a large movie library to its holdings. In 2000, Time Warner thought it was expanding its empire again by merging with the Internet service provider America Online, AOL, to become AOL Time Warner. The deal, however, was made at the height of the dot.com boom. Almost immediately, AOL's stock dropped sharply. The company lost millions on AOL, and in 2009, AOL was dropped from the company name and was spun off as a separate company. The *New York Times* noted dryly, "Trapped in a troubled marriage, AOL Time Warner decided yesterday to return to its maiden name, dropping its first three letters."[52] After all the merging and acquiring, a summary of Time Warner Communications holdings now includes the following:

- Time Inc. publications, such as *Time*, *Sports Illustrated*, and *People*;
- Home Box Office, including HBO and Cinemax;
- Time Warner Cable Company;
- Turner Broadcasting System, including CNN, TNT, TBS, Cartoon Network, and Turner Classic Movies;
- Warner Bros. Picture Group, which produces movies such as the *Harry Potter* series and *Clash of the Titans*;
- New Line Cinema, which produces movies such as *A Nightmare on Elm Street*, *Austin Powers*, *The Lord of the Rings*, and *Sex in the City*;
- Warner Bros. Television Group, with worldwide production, distribution, and broadcasting;
- Warner Music Group, Atlantic Recording, and Elektra Entertainment, which records and distributes work by artists such as Bruno Mars and Cee-lo; and
- DC Comics, which includes characters such as Superman and Batman.

NO MEDIA, NO CAPITALISM, NO GLOBALIZATION

With these oligopolistic giants in mind, I now want to consider more broadly the relationship of media and global capitalism. The title of this section is meant to be provocative. But let's consider how true it is. Without media, could modern-day capitalism exist? At every level, capitalism depends upon recent, regular, and reliable information. The fisherman needs to know how much buyers are paying for salmon as he brings his catch to market. The market buyers need to know how much others are paying and also how much food companies are willing to pay. The food company needs to know how much other companies are paying and what the grocery stores are buying. The grocery stores need to know how much other stores are paying and what consumers are buying. The consumers need to know how much others are charging before they make their purchase. And somewhere on Wall Street, stockbrokers are watching the stock price of the food company rise and fall as they decide whether to buy or sell.

Media provide economic information throughout every step of this process. Indeed, every instance of media, from cave paintings to digital media, shows the importance of gathering, recording, and communicating economic information to humans. For example, cave paintings of fish told the humans of long ago what fish might be found in nearby rivers and streams. Too, the legendary Silk Road, which you recall began around 200 BCE as a network of trade routes connecting Asia with the Mediterranean world, North Africa, and Europe, flourished as the Chinese invention of paper spread along the route. The new medium allowed permanent and portable records of debts and transactions. Similarly, the first wire services were quickly put to use for economic purposes. In a fascinating study, *Communication and Empire: Media, Markets, and Globalization, 1860–1930*, Dwayne Winseck and Robert Pike examine how the first wire services and cable companies competed to stretch cables literally around the world to establish and expand markets.[53]

Newspapers, magazines, radio, television, and the Internet have all been quickly adapted to economic globalization. Oliver Boyd-Barrett and Tehri Rantanen find that "the links between modernity, capitalism, news, news agencies and globalization are an outstanding but neglected feature of the past 150 years."[54] Today, the flow of economic data and information is instantaneous and voluminous. Around the world, media outlets, such as London's *Financial Times*; Japan's *Nihon Keizai Shimbun*; China's *Jingji Cankao Bao*; and the United States' *Bloomberg News*, *Wall Street Journal*, and CNBC, provide individuals and corporations with the information they require to buy and sell. And minute by minute, the media carry news of the slightest rise or fall of the market. As I wrote these paragraphs, news brought me word of Nike's stock price, which opened at $83.56, rose and fell in the morning to a low of $83.38, and closed at $83.80.

NO WORLD NEWS TONIGHT: THE DEMISE OF INTERNATIONAL REPORTING

Minute by minute, over the course of the day, Nike's stock price was updated. Minute by minute, over the course of the day, thousands of children died from starvation. There was no ticker for them. No news of them.

I want to return now to Robert McChesney's wise observation that the global oligopoly of media is not particularly interested in promulgating political and cultural values around the world. The oligopoly is interested in making money. We have looked at the implications for local cultures of the profit-seeking media oligopoly. Yet the oligopoly has also had a disastrous influence on news and what used to be called "public affairs reporting."

One significant consequence: The oligopoly's single-minded interest in profits results in mass content rather than local content. The most profitable content for global media will be that which can be mass produced, published, and broadcast widely and simultaneously in numerous countries, with little need for local adaptation. These include numerous reruns of U.S. shows, such as *House* and *Grey's Anatomy*; global sporting events, such as the Olympics or the World Cup; and celebrity entertainment programs, such as *Oprah*. The emphasis on mass content has direct implications for news. Rather than producing homegrown programming on public affairs and issues, local media outlets carry the mass-produced content of their conglomerate owners.

Another consequence of the single-minded pursuit of profit is cheap productions. The most profitable content will be inexpensive, non–labor intensive, and easy to produce. Reality shows, game shows, and celebrity talk shows are cheap. Local news shows, investigative reporting, and documentaries are expensive. The *Idol* franchise is a good example of a highly successful, relatively cheap production. You might be familiar with the reality television show *American Idol*, in which singers compete before judges, a local audience, and a national viewing audience. The show was adapted for America from the British hit *Pop Idol*. For years, the American adaptation was the number-one television show in the world. Too, with the success of *American Idol*, many stations around the globe created their own

Idol programs, such as *Malaysian Idol*. Other reality shows also sprang up. Besides being successful, the reality shows are inexpensive. The performers receive little compensation. The settings and scenes are undistinguished. All this *Idol* chatter, however, takes up time, space, and resources that could be devoted to public affairs.

A third consequence of profit making on media content, as McChesney and Sarikakis pointed out earlier, is that the most profitable content over the long run will be escapist and apolitical. News and political content can upset and divide the populace, drive away viewers, and displease authorities. The impact is that, around the world, news has become softer, lighter, and less challenging, with space and time given over to weather, celebrities, sensation, sports, recipes, and other less weighty fare. One scholar calls the result the "mass production of ignorance."[55] Daya Kishan Thussu spent years as a journalist in the global south. As a media scholar, he has watched with dismay the "poverty of news." Despite twenty-four-hour television news and online journalism outlets, he says that the "issues concerning the world's poor are being increasingly marginalised as a softer lifestyle variety of reporting appears to dominate global television news agendas."[56]

The media oligopoly's drive for profits thus leads to mass-produced, cheap, escapist, apolitical content—with little interest in or incentive for news. The results have been especially devastating for international news reporting. Foreign news bureaus are expensive. Training international journalists is expensive. International travel is expensive. You can guess the result. Around the world, media that once had extensive foreign correspondence have disbanded staffs and shuttered bureaus. My former employer, the *Philadelphia Inquirer*, once had more than half a dozen bureaus overseas. Now, none. U.S. television networks, such as NBC, CBS, and ABC, have all closed bureaus.

The *American Journalism Review* carried a bleak headline that told the story: "Retreating from the World: The Sharp Decline in Foreign Coverage."[57] The research was equally bleak. The magazine found that eighteen U.S. newspapers and two chains have shuttered every one of their overseas bureaus in the dozen years since the magazine first surveyed foreign coverage. "What's more," the review said, "an untold number of regional and local papers have dramatically decreased the amount of foreign news they publish. Television networks, meanwhile, slashed the time they devote to foreign news and narrowed their focus largely to war zones."[58] Years before the economic downturn that began in 2008, news reporting was scaled back and staffs were cut. A Harvard University study of U.S. network news found that in the 1970s, 45 percent of the coverage was devoted to international news. In 1995, the total was 13.5 percent.[59]

It's not just an American phenomenon. The BBC has seen hundreds of positions cut worldwide. News media in China, India, and Japan have relatively few correspondents outside their homeland. International news coverage is down around the world.[60] The irony is grim. In a time that has seen the advent of twenty-four-hour news television, the creation of the Internet, the expansion of cell phones to every village in the world, and the capacity for instantaneous reporting from every corner of the globe, we now have less international news than ever. Shahira Fahmy studied foreign affairs reporting after 9/11. Fahmy suggested that we might expect that the watershed events surrounding the terrorist bombing of the World Trade Center, and the subsequent wars in Afghanistan and Iraq, would combine with the explosion of new media to produce a wealth of coverage. The title of Fahmy's essay: "How Could So Much Produce So Little?"[61]

International events that do receive attention in news are most often dramatic, sensational, eye-catching incidents. Earthquakes, hurricanes, tsunamis, coups, terrorist attacks, celebrity deaths, and other spectacles get intense, hyperventilated coverage, which lasts only until the drama is sucked dry and the media have moved on to the next happening. Top international news stories of the last few years include the 2004 "Christmas tsunami" in Asia, the 2005 Hurricane Katrina that devastated New Orleans, the 2009 death of Michael Jackson, the 2010 earthquake in Haiti, and the 2011 revolution in Egypt. These dramatic events attracted hundreds of reporters and weeks of coverage, often nonstop. Other occurrences during that period? From the standpoint of the news, it's as if they never happened.

IGNORING THE BOTTOM BILLION AND THE MEGACITY

I understand the interest and appeal of dramatic and sensational stories. Millions of people rightly follow the coverage of revolutions, tsunamis, hurricanes, and earthquakes. The infinite capacities of the Internet and twenty-four-hour news stations allow room for such coverage. The problem comes because other stories are *not* covered—stories also with great import and impact, but lacking the easy sensationalism required by the media oligopoly. Two stories in particular roil our planet every day and yet scarcely merit coverage.

Paul Collier, a professor of economics at Oxford University, has given an apt title to the first story: "the Bottom Billion." Globalization, Collier writes, has helped bring about an economic marvel. Not too long ago, five billion of the world's six billion people lived in poverty. Today, primarily because of advances in China, India, and other parts of Asia, the numbers are reversed: one billion of the world's six billion people live in poverty. The turnaround is remarkable. But it's also distressing. How, in this world of great plenty, can a billion people still be living in dire poverty? These bottom billion, primarily in Africa and Central Asia, "are falling behind, and often falling apart," Collier says. "The countries at the bottom coexist with the twenty-first century, but their reality is the fourteenth century: civil war, plague, ignorance."[62]

The bottom billion deserve coverage for basic humanitarian reasons. But the bottom billion also deserve coverage for journalistic reasons. In the parlance of news, the bottom billion are a *good story*. The nations are sites for the world's most critical issues. Some of the nations, such as Somalia, do not have stable governments and have become grounds where terrorists can freely live, train, and work. Many of the nations have huge troves of natural resources that are being pirated by crime syndicates, drug cartels, and terrorists. Environmental issues abound. Many of the nations are also sites for heroic medical research that could lead to the elimination of malaria and AIDS. The people of the bottom billion make compelling subjects as they struggle against odds unknown to most of the world. In short, the bottom billion could be a gripping, powerful story, yet the stories do not fit the cheap, easy, escapist, apolitical model imposed by the media oligopoly. Thus the bottom billion live and die in a dark corner of the global village.

Another story that is transforming our planet daily is the growth of cities, especially what have been called "megacities," cities of more than ten million people. In 1800, our world was rural. Most people lived on farmlands and plains. Just 3 percent of the population lived in cities. In 1900, 13 percent lived in cities. In 2010, the world reached a milestone: more than half the people of the world now live in cities. The editors of the *World Policy Journal* nicely noted the extraordinary moment:

> Since the dawn of recorded time, when mankind first gathered in the Fertile Crescent ten millennia before Christ, cities have served as the core, indeed the cradle of civilization. In cities, men and women have always gathered together for protection, productivity and, ultimately, creativity. From the city we may trace the very development of humanity. Today, it is the attractions of our urban conglomerations that prove to be all but irresistible magnets—vast populations are migrating on a scale never before seen in human history.[63]

This gradual transformation of our world from rural to urban surely deserves continued focus from the news. No area of life—from health to the environment to entertainment to transportation to family life—is being untouched. The rise of the megacity is already literally changing the face of the world. Astronauts now document this changing face by photographing the Earth at night. Their pictures show the ever-growing knots of city lights with the lacelike networks that connect them across more and more of the planet.[64]

The City Mayor Foundation has studied the population growth of urban areas—which includes the city and the sprawling metropolis around the city limits. For 2006, the foundation identified Tokyo as the largest urban area, with 35.53 million people. Mexico City was next, with just under 20 million.[65] The foundation's forecast for 2020 was striking. Tokyo would still reign with 37 million people—not much of a change since there is little room for growth—but now eight other cities are projected to have more than 20 million people: Mumbai, Delhi, Dhaka, Mexico City, Sao Paolo, Lagos, Jakarta, and New York.[66]

Already most of those cities have seen huge slums and shantytowns appear almost overnight. Daily, people flee the poverty, danger, disease, and unrest of their rural villages—only to find more of the same in the city. The journal *Foreign Policy* published a stirring photo essay on what it called "arrival cities." Here is how that essay began:

> Within the city is another city, located on the periphery of our vision and beyond the tourist maps. It has become the setting of the world's next chapter, driven by exertion and promise, battered by violence and death, strangled by neglect and misunderstanding. History is being written, and largely ignored, in places like Liu Gong Li on the fringes of Chongqing, in Clichy-sous-Bois on the outskirts of Paris, in the almost million-strong arrival city of Dharavi in Mumbai, and in Compton on the edge of Los Angeles—all places settled by people who have arrived from the village, all places that function to propel people into the core life of the city and to send support back to the next wave of arrivals. These places are known around the world by many names: as the slums, favelas, bustees, bidonvilles, ashwaiyyat, shantytowns, kampongs, urban villages, gecekondular, and barrios of the developing world, but also as the immigrant neighborhoods, ethnic districts, banlieues difficiles, Plattenbau developments, Chinatowns, Little Indias, Hispanic quarters, urban slums, and migrant suburbs of wealthy countries, which are themselves each year absorbing 2 million people, mainly villagers, from the developing world.[67]

That eloquent and disturbing paragraph attempts to capture the massive dislocation and realignment of the world's population. These cities will have far-reaching consequences at the local and global level. How can such consequences not be newsworthy? And, as if more drama were needed, Mike Davis forecasts a "planet of slums." He writes,

> Thus, the cities of the future, rather than being made out of glass and steel as envisioned by earlier generations of urbanists, are instead largely constructed out of crude brick, straw, recycled plastic, cement blocks, and scrap wood. Instead of cities of light soaring toward heaven, much of the twenty-first-century urban world squats in squalor, surrounded by pollution, excrement, and decay.[68]

That is beautiful writing. Instead of urban towers of glass and steel, modern cities are being constructed of scrap wood and straw. How can attention not be paid? Slow, incremental change is difficult for the media to document and report. Yet the transformation of the face of the world would seem to be of interest even to the media oligopoly whose executive suites look down upon many of these teeming cities. But for now, the urbanization of the global village proceeds with little attention from the media oligopoly.

MO AMIN: A SPOTLIGHT ON THE BOTTOM BILLION

The 1984 famine in Ethiopia had reached desperate days. Throughout the year, the rains had rarely come. Farmlands had turned to dust. Rivers and streams had run dry. The people of Ethiopia who depended on the land and water for their very livelihood were frantic. The government was of little assistance. Rebel groups were fighting government troops on a number of fronts. Resettlement of populations and other government policies to counter the insurgents had failed and led to food shortages and dislocated people. Government attention and resources were directed to the rebellion. The people, more than eight million, were left to starve.

With no other recourse, many people simply packed their few belongings and left. They headed out in search of food, water, and aid. They gathered in huge crowds of death and despair. Hundreds of thousands were dying in the dust. Local chapters of international relief agencies began hearing of the catastrophe. But travel through the war-torn land was hazardous and sometimes impossible. Few outside of Ethiopia knew of the ongoing disaster.[69]

Mohamed "Mo" Amin was an African photojournalist. Born in Nairobi, he developed an early love for photography and dropped out of school to pursue work for newspapers, magazines, and wire services. He knew the continent, and he was fearless. He was able to get stories and pictures throughout the continent when others could not. He reported on political upheavals and coups. He chronicled the Cold War politics by the United States and Soviet Union in Africa. He founded his own photojournalism agency and added news video to his output. Amin's work became a primary source of African news for Western media, from the BBC to the *New York Times*.[70]

Amin learned of the famine in Ethiopia but had no idea of its dramatic scope. Still, he worked tirelessly to navigate through the civil war zones and report the crisis. When he finally reached one of the huge encampments of people, he was stunned at what he found: a landscape of death and dying with a ghastly soundtrack of moaning and crying. He worked feverishly. He captured nightmare images of stick children with vacant eyes and emaciated limbs, weeping mothers clutching long-dead babies, and rotting corpses covered with flies. He was able to get his photographs and videos out through the war zones and into the hands of Western media.[71]

The first broadcast of Amin's reporting, narrated by the BBC's Michael Buerk, shocked Britain. Government and charity groups leapt into action. Amin's work was used by other media around the world. Huge mobilization efforts were undertaken to supply aid. As if in reaction to previous disinterest, the waves of charity built. British music producer Bob Geldof saw Buerk's report and was inspired to gather local musicians to raise funds for famine relief. Within weeks, some of the United Kingdom's most famous musicians, including Bono, Phil Collins, Boy George, George Michael, and others, had recorded the song "Do They Know It's Christmas?"—just in time for Christmas sales. The record sold more than a million copies in one week, with all proceeds donated to the Ethiopian famine.[72]

Still the charitable wave continued. Inspired by the success of the British effort, American musicians joined together to record their own charity relief single. The song "We Are the World" was written by Michael Jackson and Lionel Richie and recorded by the biggest names in American rock and pop music, including Bob Dylan, Ray Charles, Billy Joel, Diana Ross, Cyndi Lauper, Bruce Springsteen, Stevie Wonder, Willie Nelson, Smokey Robinson, and many more. The song became the fastest-selling American pop single in history.[73]

And still the charitable efforts did not stop. Geldof planned for two concerts to be held simultaneously in London and Philadelphia. The event, Live Aid, was to be broadcast around the world. Again, the biggest names in music took the stage for daylong concerts. The broadcast remains one of the largest satellite-linked television broadcasts ever. Two billion people, perhaps one-third of the world, across sixty nations, watched the live broadcast. In between performances, viewers were educated about the famine and instructed on how to donate to manned phone lines around the world.[74] And some of the photos and videos that played across the screen were the work of Mo Amin, who had helped to start it all.

Though coverage of the Ethiopian famine was the highlight of his career, Amin continued to report the triumphs and tribulations of his home continent. In 1991, an explosion at an ammunition dump blew off his left arm. Undeterred, Amin had a prosthetic arm attached to his body so he could continue his work. Sadly and ironically, Amin died in an Ethiopian airliner. Hijackers took over a jet on which he was a passenger. Amin was killed when the plane crash-landed in waters off Africa.[75]

An international reporting group said this of Amin:

> His coverage of the 1984 Ethiopian famine proved so compelling that it inspired a collective global conscience and the greatest act of giving in the 20th century. He and his work served as both the inspiration and as a catalyst for We Are the World/USA for Africa; Live Aid; Heal the World and Live 8. His reporting shamed the world into action and undoubtedly rescued a country from absolute destruction by famine.[76]

Africa's misery continues. Debate goes on about how best to battle its poverty, starvation, and disease. But the work of Mo Amin shows us that people can be inspired to help others in the global village. The media oligopoly can be forced to pay heed and use its massive power for good. People can react as concerned citizens rather than contented consumers. Some credit can go to Mo Amin.

6

MEDIA AND POLITICAL GLOBALIZATION

Killing Stories—and Journalists

Investigative journalist Anna Politkovskaya reported fearlessly about Russian military abuses in Chechnya, including the torture and abduction of civilians by Russian soldiers. On a Saturday afternoon, she came home with groceries to her Moscow apartment building, stepped into the elevator, and was shot to death. She had two gunshot wounds—one to the head.

Said Tahlil Ahmed was a popular radio journalist for Horn Afrik in Mogadishu, Somalia. On his radio show in early 2009, Ahmed discussed the tense presidential elections contested by moderate and militant Islamic parties. Not long after, as Ahmed walked through the Bakara Market in Mogadishu, masked gunmen circled and shot him repeatedly, killing him instantly. He was survived by his wife and eight children.

Lasantha Wickramatunga, editor in chief of the weekly newspaper *The Sunday Leader*, was a thoughtful, relentless critic of the Sri Lankan government. Even after death threats, he continued reporting and writing. One morning, as he drove to work, eight helmeted men on four motorcycles surrounded his car and shot him to death.[1]

MEDIA AND POLITICS IN THE GLOBAL VILLAGE

An essential process of globalization is political. Globalization has transformed world politics in profound ways. It led to the formation and then the overthrow of kingdoms and empires. It led to the creation of the nation-state. And now some argue that the nation-state is being weakened as people and borders become ever more fluid in our globalized world. Some argue that *trans*national political actors, from NGOs like Greenpeace to corporations to the United Nations, now rise in prominence in our age of globalization.

When we add the media to the admixture of globalization and politics, we touch upon some key features of life in the global village of Babel. This chapter will consider three of the marked outcomes that arise from the current era of media and political globalization.

- Of utmost importance, though media corporations are themselves powerful political actors, individual journalists are subject to brutal and intense intimidation as more actors contend for power in the global village. There has never been a more dangerous time to work in media.
- We will also see that the media are subject to other pressures in this age of high-tech persuasion, manipulation, and propaganda. Economic, political, and personal pressures shape the news around the globe.
- Finally, we will consider a more hopeful question for the future: whether new media have the potential to invigorate and transform political life in the global village.

KILLING JOURNALISTS: THE WORLD AS WAR ZONE

I began this chapter with three brief reports on the killing of journalists. I could have included hundreds. The International Federation of Journalists (IFJ) estimates that more than 1,100 journalists and media workers have been killed in the line of duty over the last twelve years.[2] They died in war zones. They died from car bombs. They died covering earthquakes, floods, and hurricanes. They died in drug raids. Perhaps five hundred of them, though, were specifically targeted, hunted down, and murdered because of their work.

More troubling, the journalists die without justice. The Committee to Protect Journalists (CPJ) estimates that less than 15 percent of the murders of journalists are solved or prosecuted.[3] It is the ultimate form of censorship. The voice of the journalist is forever silenced. The intimidating message chills newsrooms far and wide. And no one pays a price.

Mexico, Russia, and the Philippines top the list of places where journalists are slaughtered with impunity. Each nation displays the new array of forces now threatening journalists in the global village. In Mexico, drug cartels brazenly target journalists who dare to report on their trafficking and their murderous wars against the police and rival cartels. In Russia, journalists who report on the separatist movement in Chechnya, such as Anna Politkovskaya, have been tracked down and killed by loyalists of the Russian military as well as the Chechens. Journalists who seek to uncover extensive fraud in Russian government and business are also targeted. In the Philippines, journalists covering political rivalry and conflict are always at risk. In the single worst mass killing of journalists on record, for example, twenty-seven reporters were killed.[4] They were covering a group of civilians registering a candidate in an upcoming election. The entire group, including the journalists, was massacred.

It did not used to be this way. Though journalists were sometimes targeted because of their reporting on organized crime or drugs, the assassination of a journalist was relatively rare and was met by public outcry. Journalists were primarily at physical risk in war zones. Now, in our age of globalization, the entire world can be a war zone. Numerous forces compete for wealth and power, within and across borders, including governments, state militias, paramilitary groups, political parties, drug cartels, religious organizations, insurgents, corporations, terrorists, and others. All these groups can be threatened by the work of a crusading reporter. All have targeted reporters. The global village is a harrowing place for journalists.

THE BEHEADING OF DANIEL PEARL

The kidnapping and killing of Daniel Pearl has come to symbolize for many people the heightened dangers for journalists working in the global village. His death was horrific. Born in 1964, Pearl graduated from Stanford as a communications major. He traveled extensively and worked himself up through the journalism ranks to become the South Asia bureau chief for the *Wall Street Journal*. In 2002, Pearl was in Karachi, Pakistan, investigating possible ties between a Pakistani religious leader and Richard Reid, the infamous "shoe bomber" who had tried to blow up a jet with a bomb hidden in his shoe. Pearl thought he had arranged an interview with the Pakistani cleric. It was a trap.[5]

Pearl was kidnapped by a militant group with links to al-Qaeda. The group noted Pearl's Jewish heritage, called him a CIA operative, and sent the United States a list of demands for Pearl's release, including the freeing of all Pakistanis arrested on terrorism charges. Photographs of Pearl were included. He was handcuffed and holding up a newspaper. A gun was at his head. The U.S. government, Pearl's editor, and Pearl's wife, pregnant with their first child, pleaded for his life.

Not long after, a hideous video was released to the media, its title "The Slaughter of the Spy-Journalist, the Jew Daniel Pearl." It shows Pearl with his throat slit. It shows Pearl's head being cut from his body by a man's hand. It shows the hand holding Pearl's head by the hair as demands are read.

The world was repulsed and outraged. Pearl's body was later found, cut into ten pieces and buried in a shallow grave north of Karachi. His kidnappers were eventually arrested. The identity of his murderer remained unclear. However, Khalid Sheikh Mohammed, in U.S. custody for possibly masterminding the September 11, 2001, attacks on the United States, confessed to the murder. Researchers conducted vein-matching analysis on Mohammed's hands and the hand in the beheading video. They concluded that Mohammed was indeed Pearl's killer.[6]

Pearl's death has remained a galvanizing force for those concerned with press freedom. The Daniel Pearl Foundation was formed by family and friends in honor of Pearl's journalistic mission. Daniel Pearl World Music Days have been held worldwide since 2002. Mariane Pearl, his widow, wrote a memoir of her life with him, *A Mighty Heart*. The book eventually became a film starring Dan Futterman and Angelina Jolie. An HBO documentary, *The Journalist and the Jihadi: The Murder of Daniel Pearl*, was narrated by international correspondent Christiane Amanpour and was nominated for two Emmy Awards. And in 2010, U.S. President Barack Obama signed the "Daniel Pearl Freedom of the Press Act," which seeks to protect journalists around the world.

UNESCO AND FREEDOM OF EXPRESSION

Numerous organizations have taken up the plight of journalists, including CPJ, IFJ, Reporters without Borders, and the Inter American Press Association. UNESCO—the United Nations Educational, Scientific and Cultural Organization—has particular prominence. It is the UN organization devoted to the protection of freedom of expression, the free flow of ideas, and access to organization and knowledge. We will see in the next chapter that UNESCO has been a site of controversy and contest in the arena of media and cultural globalization. But on the subject of the protection of journalists amid political globalization, UNESCO has attempted to rise to the challenge. Its headquarters in Paris has a huge stone on the site engraved with lines from the preamble to UNESCO's constitution, in ten languages: "Since wars begin in the minds of men, it is in the minds of men that the defences of peace must be constructed."

Hélène-Marie Gosselin had worked with the United Nations since 1979 before joining UNESCO in 1993. As director of the liaison office between UNESCO and the UN, she was looking forward to work that promoted peace, cultural interaction, and the flowering of journalism. But from her first days, her work was shadowed by the murder of journalists. "In all of my time with the UN and UNESCO," Gosselin told me in an interview, "I have never seen a more dangerous time for journalists." Her voice dropped almost to a whisper. "It is the worst I have ever seen. Almost every day . . ."[7]

Gosselin attributed the rise in the killing of journalists to profound political changes wrought by globalization. In the past, when journalists were primarily at risk in war zones, conflicts were defined and managed between nation-states, she said. Dangerous places were easily identified. And even on the battlefield, reporters were often treated like humanitarian aid workers and were sometimes given free passage back and forth from front lines. Their reporting was not seen as a risk to either side. "The journalist," Gosselin said, "was not a threat to a nation at war. The journalist was an observer."

Now, she noted, conflicts are often not between nations but between groups within nations. The conflicts are in ill-defined areas between ill-defined groups. They can occur across borders, as with drug-trafficking gangs. They can occur within villages or towns, such as battles between factions, rival ethnic groups, or extremist political parties. Their conflicts are not wars but murder, retribution, genocide, and internecine warfare. In all these cases, news reporting can be threatening—to drug running, to illicit trafficking, to ethnic sensitivities, to religious zealotry, or to political positions. "In all these cases," Gosselin said, "the journalist, they feel, can be an enemy."

Gosselin pointed to civil war in Somalia in the 1990s as a key moment "when the gloves came off" in attacks on journalists as well as humanitarian workers and aid officials. Revolutionary forces, counterrevolutionary forces, peacekeepers, and profit makers all contended for control in the fractured nation. In such chaos, roles and titles were meaningless, and few people were safe. Journalists, UN peacekeepers, and humanitarian workers were viewed as possible infiltrators or partners with enemy forces. They were attacked and killed. "It did not matter who you were or what you were trying to do," Gosselin said.

In other lands, Gosselin said, the killing of journalists arises not from chaos but from a systematic attempt to eliminate those with the ability to inform the populace. She identified the Khmer Rouge in Cambodia and the Taliban in Afghanistan as two groups that engaged in conscious campaigns of extermination. "They wanted to wipe out intellectuals and others who might be a political and ideological threat," Gosselin said. "Journalists help inform public opinion, and so they have especially been targets." Reporters seeking to inform the public of corporate and political corruption in other lands are hunted too.

Under such conditions, Gosselin said, the role of UNESCO is to protect journalists when possible and to protest their persecution at local, state, and global levels. She said she was humbled by the commitment. "The journalists are very brave to work under such circumstances," Gosselin concluded. "People just do not know what they face."

KILLING STORIES TO SAVE JOURNALISTS

Luis Carlos Santiago, a photographer for *El Diario de Juarez*, the daily newspaper in Ciudad Juarez, Mexico, was killed in a city parking lot by gunmen thought to be working for drug cartels. He was just twenty-one. He was the second *El Diario* journalist killed in two years. The day after Santiago's death, *El Diario* editors published a stunning, plaintive, front-page editorial to the drug gangs titled "What Do You Want from Us?" The editorial said, "It is impossible for us to do our job under these conditions. Tell us what you expect from us as a newspaper?"[8]

When I was working as a reporter, we had a term when a story was halted, shelved, or otherwise not published. We said the story was "killed." Journalists killed stories for a variety of reasons, including lack of confirmation or lack of interest and importance. In our cruel, lethal era, however, when journalists are slain with impunity, killing stories has become more commonplace. Journalists kill stories to avoid being killed. Self-censorship by journalists is an unfortunate by-product of these murderous times.

Journalists in Mexico face extraordinary pressures covering what one writer called "the global economy's new killing fields."[9] Drug cartels have amassed incredible wealth and power. They prepare, buy, and sell marijuana, cocaine, heroin, and other narcotics worldwide. The cartels protect their trade—from Mexican authorities, international agencies, and each other—with shocking displays of violence. Judges, police, government officials, federal agents, and more are routinely tortured and killed. Their bodies are hung or displayed as warnings or messages to others. The cartels influence every aspect of political, cultural, and economic life in Mexico.[10] Reporting on the cartels is essential—yet fraught with danger.

Even before the death of Santiago, Reporters without Borders had published a report entitled "Self-Censorship, Exile or Certain Death: The Choice Faced by Journalists in Ciudad Juárez."[11] Ricardo Trotti, a writer for *Global Journalist*, noted, "A popular saying preaches that a thief lets the victim choose between 'money or life,' but in Mexico, the dilemma faced by a journalist is a lot more cruel. It is either self-censorship or death."[12]

The seeming capitulation of *El Diario* to the drug cabal of Juarez galvanized the country. High-level discussions began on the increasing intimidation of Mexican journalists. UNESCO protested the continued killings. The Committee to Protect Journalists and the Inter American Press Association held an emergency meeting the following week with President Felipe Calderón and then brought Mexican journalists together for a conference on self-censorship and the drug cartels.

The conference confirmed the coercion of journalists across the country. Editor Patricia Mercado told the group that drug traffickers have "almost become news editors."[13] She said she had endured years of threats and intimidation from drug cartels. Not long before the conference, she said, she received an extraordinary demand from a cartel: run a story written by the group, or someone in the newsroom would be kidnapped. Mercado ran the prepared story. It told the tale of an innocent young man killed by the army. The story was designed to foster mistrust in the army, the enemy of the cartel. Mercado had no apologies. "If it's a question of life or death, I have no trouble making a decision. The lives of my reporters are most important."[14]

The Mexican journalists discussed ways they might continue their work. For example, they considered covering sensitive stories without bylines. They discussed reporting on the cartels collectively and running the stories at the same time in numerous publications throughout the country. The cartels perhaps would have too many subjects for revenge under such a method. A similar plan had been tried in Colombia. Those methods are now underway. Yet despite the attention, conferences, and methods, Mexico remains a menacing place for journalists in the global village.

KILLING STORIES TO MANUFACTURE CONSENT

For a few years in international communication studies, scholars pursued what was called "the CNN effect." According to the CNN effect, foreign policy—especially the actions of the U.S. government—seemed to be driven by dominant stories appearing on CNN and other twenty-four-hour news networks. That is, the theory went, if CNN was devoting nonstop attention to tumult in Somalia, U.S. government officials would feel public pressure to intervene in Somalia. Media seemed to be driving some foreign policy.[15] The concept seemed logical and attracted some interest. But eventually other scholars pursued the CNN effect in earnest, testing and retesting its hypothesis. For them, the concept did not hold up to scrutiny. Policy making, they found, was driven by numerous factors, and the news was not often of primary importance or consequence to the decision making of policy makers.[16]

In fact, in era after era, the opposite hypothesis appears to be true: governments shape and manipulate the news. It is another key feature of media and political globalization. Officials around the world are extremely successful at influencing and molding the news so that it builds support for their domestic and foreign policies. All of humankind's considerable persuasive techniques—from cajoling to coddling to conniving to coercing—are put into play so that news media report favorably on government actions and initiatives.

In Mexico, stories are killed so that journalists might live to see another day. Too often, however, journalists kill stories for less honorable reasons, and journalists must bear some of the responsibility for lax coverage of government and society. Bribery of journalists, for example, remains a fact of life in many countries. In a report, "Cash for Coverage: Bribery of Journalists around the World," the Center for Media Assistance calls bribes "the dark part of journalism." According to the report, "Not only do journalists accept bribes and media houses accept paid material disguised as news stories, but all too often, reporters and editors are the perpetrators, extorting money either for publishing favorable stories—or for not publishing damaging ones."[17] In Africa, the practice has a name: "brown envelope journalism."[18]

In many other places, however, the influence and inducements are subtler. Stories are killed or produced so that journalists might maintain good relations with government and corporate officials or so that they might attain or maintain status, perks, and prestige. In a now classic but still contested study, Edward Herman and Noam Chomsky charge the news media with being complicit in "manufacturing consent."[19] The authors challenge the standard conception of Western journalists as "watchdogs" on the powerful. Rather, they say, news media too often fill the classic function of government and corporate propaganda.

Outright bribes seldom influence coverage, Herman and Chomsky say. Instead, structural factors shape reporting: the media's ownership by, or close relationship with, corporations; the drive for profits from circulations, ratings, and advertising revenue; and journalists' close relationships with biased or involved sources in government and business.[20] These forces, the authors say, can lead to the routine publishing and promoting of news shaped by governments and corporations. Herman and Chomsky's propaganda model shows "the routes by which money and power are able to filter out the news fit to print, marginalize dissent, and allow the government and dominant private interests to get their messages across to the public."[21]

The dangers of such a relationship are especially acute if a government attempts to build a case to go to war. It is perhaps the most critical decision a nation can make. Citizens will be asked to die—and to kill—for the sake of the war. In nations where the media are under the strict, repressive control of the government, state-sponsored journalists are pressed to follow the government line, demonize the enemy, and make the case for conflict. In countries with a freer press, the process is more subtle, but often no less effective.

One of the most important decisions made by the United States in the twenty-first century was the 2003 invasion of Iraq. Tens of thousands of Iraqis and Americans have been killed, and the social, political, cultural, and economic consequences of the invasion will last deep into the century. As you might expect, I was enormously interested in the reporting that led up to this war. In the section below, I will provide the results of a case study I undertook of U.S. news reporting in the months before the 2003 invasion of Iraq. Though my inquiry was on the 2003 decision to go to war, the same questions can and should be asked anytime a nation goes to war. What are the rationales given by leaders for the war? How do the news media report, judge, and weigh those rationales?

NEWS AND THE RATIONALES FOR WAR IN IRAQ

The September 11 attacks on the World Trade Center and Pentagon of course were a defining moment for the United States and its foreign policy. The administration of President George W. Bush at first responded with the invasion of Afghanistan. The original rationale for that invasion was that Osama bin Laden and the terrorist group al-Qaeda, who were thought to be behind the September 11 attacks, were living and training in Afghanistan with the approval of that country's leaders, the Taliban. The U.S. invasion was intended to remove the rulers of Afghanistan, disperse al-Qaeda, and attempt to capture bin Laden.[22]

Not long after that invasion, in the first months of 2003, the Bush administration attempted to build support, nationally and internationally, for war against Iraq. Through speeches, press conferences, committee reports, United Nations sessions, televised addresses, and other venues, the president and his spokespeople offered rationales for war. Saddam Hussein, the president said, had weapons of mass destruction and was a threat to U.S. and world security. Saddam was linked to terrorism, particularly the activities of al-Qaeda. Saddam was a despotic ruler over the people of Iraq. Saddam was an impediment to peace in the Middle East.[23]

Others were unconvinced. Members of the UN Security Council, including France, Russia, and Germany, argued for a process of inspection and eventual destruction of Iraqi weapons and refused to pass a war resolution. Other U.S. allies, too, were not persuaded of the need for war. In early March, millions of people held peace protests in cities around the world. The Bush administration, allied with leaders of Britain and Spain, pressed forward. On March 19, U.S. jets bombed Baghdad and war began.

How did U.S. news media report events in the crucial weeks before war with Iraq? In a democratic country, the news media should play a vital role in the decision-making process. As a nation prepares for war, the news media should offer sites in which rationales for war are identified and verified; official claims are solicited and evaluated; alternate views are sought and assessed; costs, both human and material, are weighed; legalities are established; possible outcomes and aftermaths are considered; and wide-ranging debates are given voice. The consequences of war seem to require no less from the news.[24]

METAPHORS OF WAR

In the chapter on language, we saw that many scholars feel metaphor is integral to human understanding, an inescapable aspect of human thought. Neither good nor bad, metaphor may be the only way for humans to comprehend profound and complex issues, such as life, death, sickness, health, war, and peace.[25] Metaphor provides an excellent means of analyzing U.S. news coverage of events from 2003.[26]

There is no way, of course, to study the literally millions of stories of U.S. news on the war. Faced with this situation, researchers thus must choose a smaller sample to analyze. To study metaphor in news reporting before the Iraq war, I chose *NBC Nightly News*. At the time of the research, *NBC Nightly News* was the most watched U.S. evening news show, averaging close to twelve million viewers nightly. I used the time period of February 5, 2003, the day of Secretary of State Colin Powell's report to the

UN Security Council laying out the Bush administration's rationale for war with Iraq, to March 19, 2003, the day bombs first fell on Baghdad. Broadcasts were studied nightly, and transcripts were obtained for each newscast. More than four hundred reports were aired over the six-week period. Of that total, forty stories—10 percent—concerned the possible war with Iraq, a significant percentage that reflected the importance of the subject.

In that time period, reporting focused on a number of topics: the United States and Britain pressed for a UN Security Council resolution for war with Iraq; inspectors were trying to ascertain if Iraq possessed "weapons of mass destruction"; other members of the Security Council, particularly France, Germany, and Russia, were attempting to provide more time for inspections; the United States and Britain continued to build up forces in the Persian Gulf; and President Bush and his administration were attempting to build support for the war among the American people. How did *NBC Nightly News* report on all this?

Framing Metaphors

Like other networks and cable television broadcasts, *NBC Nightly News* first employed an overarching theme to introduce, promote, and organize its newscasts on the buildup for war with Iraq. These themes, a staple of broadcast news, are often spoken dramatically by news anchors or appear on the screen as banners accompanied by a vivid soundtrack or martial music. The opening themes provide an encompassing framework or structure for stories to come.

In early 2003, for example, MSNBC introduced its Iraq coverage with the words "Showdown with Saddam." CNN used "Showdown: Iraq," while Fox offered "Target Iraq: Disarming Saddam." For the time period studied, *NBC Nightly News* alternated a variety of themes and banners, including "Countdown: Iraq," "Showdown: Iraq," and, most often, "Target: Iraq." It might be easy to overlook or dismiss these themes, banners, and logos. But they are important organizing devices to which cable and broadcast networks devote considerable editorial, design, and marketing consideration.[27]

Let's look closely at the words used by NBC. A *countdown* of course is an audible backward counting, from an arbitrary starting number to zero, to mark time before an event. It can also mean the preparations carried out during the count and before the event. Of particular interest to this study, a countdown *assumes* that the upcoming event is scheduled and inevitable. A countdown moves inexorably to its conclusion.[28] By using "Countdown: Iraq" as a structural metaphor, particularly in the middle of February 2003, *NBC Nightly News* suggested the inevitability of conflict with Iraq at a time when many Americans and nations around the world were still attempting to prevent the conflict. You can see why the choice of the word *countdown* caught my attention.

Showdown was used eighteen times during the time period. "Showdown: Iraq" frames the situation as a dramatic, final confrontation, a reckoning between Iraq and an unnamed opponent—the United States? The world? The metaphor has links to American Western texts, in which two gunmen face off. In this perspective, the metaphor perhaps complements the portrayals of President George Bush as a cowboy figure. For example, a report on February 9 referred to a "crucial week in the showdown with Saddam."[29] A February 15 newscast stated that President Bush was considering "his next move in the showdown with Saddam Hussein." *Showdown* also has linguistic roots in card games, especially the placing of poker hands face up on a table to determine the winner. From any root, the metaphor suggested that the situation in Iraq seemed inevitably headed toward confrontation—a showdown. Finally, *target*. As a noun, *target* implies that Iraq is a place or object selected for military attack, especially by aerial bombing or missile assault. As a verb, *target* can be seen as a command to identify, mark, and aim at Iraq. As noun or verb, "Target: Iraq" anticipates, assumes, and metaphorically takes up conflict with Iraq. Like the other framing metaphors, *target* is aggressive and anticipates the war assumed to be coming.

Metaphors to Go to War By

Structural metaphors provided the overarching themes to NBC broadcasts. Within individual stories each night, other metaphoric language was used as the news anchors and reporters strove to make sense of events for viewers. Each report, of course, might have drawn upon a huge store of figurative language. My analysis revealed, however, a surprisingly limited cluster of metaphors in reporting the prelude to war with Iraq. Four metaphors in particular dominated reporting, connecting coverage night after night: the *timetable*, the *games of Saddam* the *patience of the White House*, and *making the case/selling the plan*.

The Timetable

NBC Nightly News referred often to *a timetable for war* that was controlling the situation between the United States and Iraq. The language of *time* pervaded broadcasts. Some of this language came directly from the

Bush administration, whose officials spoke often of *deadlines* and of Saddam *running out of time*. Newscasts adopted and extended such language. For example, on February 17, after worldwide protests against military action, a report stated, "The U.S. reassesses its *timetable for war*." The following day, the newscast said, "*The timetable for war* has been slowed by the epic diplomatic struggle between the United States and others on the UN Security Council." The metaphor could be seen in numerous other reports. "So *the clock does seem to be ticking faster* on two fronts tonight," said a February 26 story. On March 4: "Target Iraq: *The shifting timetable.* Will the U.S. skip the UN and attack Saddam within days?" In that same broadcast, a story asked, "So what is *the timeline* for war?"

The implications of *timetable* and *deadline* went unquestioned by the newscast. Anchors and reporters did not pursue the rationale behind a timetable or deadline for war. Legitimate questions might have been asked: Why set a deadline? What was its purpose? Why name a particular date? Why not wait, as other nations had urged? Rather, the timetable and deadline proved to be convenient and dramatic devices for network coverage.

The Games of Saddam

In the portrayals offered by *NBC Nightly News*, the timetable for war was threatened by the *games of Saddam*. The metaphor actually combines two tropes—*games* and *Saddam*. Metaphors of games and sports appear often in U.S. news. In the sense employed by *NBC Nightly News, games* refer to children's diversions or card games. The *game* metaphor was applied to Iraqi actions during weapons inspections and preparations for the possibility of war. The Iraqis were *playing games*.

Saddam is another metaphor—for all of Iraq. In linguistic terms, *Saddam* was the metonymic replacement of a ruler for the entire state. Metonymy is understood here as a figure of speech in which a word or phrase is substituted for another with which it is closely associated. With the *games of Saddam*, therefore, Saddam Hussein was said to be playing hide and seek with weapons of mass destruction during inspections. He was bluffing the United States and the United Nations, as if in a poker game. He was gambling with his future and the future of his people.

For example, on February 9, a story stated, "President Bush kept up the pressure on Iraq today, accusing Saddam Hussein of playing *a game of hide and seek* with weapons of mass destruction." The words *hide and seek* came from the reporter rather than the president. March 21 saw the same words: "U.S. military intelligence sources say the Iraqis have played *a game of hide and seek*, firing mobile launchers in southern Iraq even as American forces invade." Reports of March 1 and 2 referred to Saddam's "*game of deception*." Other reports cast Saddam's actions as *card games*. For example, on February 24, anchor Tom Brokaw said, "Tonight the great debate about Iraq resembles *a three-handed game of showdown poker with Saddam now sitting at the table playing his cards out in the open*."

The *games of Saddam* personalizes, dramatizes, and perhaps trivializes the weeks of negotiation that preceded the war with Iraq. The metaphor also continues the theme of *the showdown*. We have reached the finale, the showdown, of a card game, with Saddam Hussein at the table against President Bush, the United States, and the world. The metaphor also offers a sinister depiction of the Iraqi leader. It portrays Saddam Hussein as a ruler willing to treat war as a game, playing with the future of his country and the region, and gambling with the lives of his people. Tragically, U.S. forces later found that Hussein was not playing a game. Iraq did not have weapons of mass destruction.

The Patience of the White House

Another important metaphor on *NBC Nightly News* represented the weeks before war as a time that tested the *patience of the White House*. The metaphor suggested that *the White House was losing patience* with the negotiation process, the United Nations, and its allies. This metaphor also combines two tropes. The *White House* is another metonymy; it replaces President Bush and his administration with the building. The metaphor then personalizes the metonymy by attributing *patience* to the building. It seems natural until you think about it: a big white building losing patience. That's the power of metaphor.

Early in the period studied, on February 7, a report said, "President Bush, *impatient with the United Nations*, said today it better make up its mind soon about whether to side with the United States." Throughout the month, the metaphor continued to be used. The lead report on March 9 stated, "For weeks now, the White House has said it wanted to give diplomacy a chance. Well, now it appears that *the White House's patience is running out*." Other reports drew upon similar language. On February 9, the newscast cited White House impatience and stated, "Mr. Bush also said the United Nations *must soon decide whether it's going to be relevant*." The introduction to the broadcast of February 13 was "Countdown Iraq: The eve of the weapons inspectors' report; President Bush *tells the UN to show some backbone*."

The metaphor of *the patience of the White House* surely personalizes the prelude to war but also casts the Bush administration in an authoritative, almost paternal role in relation to Iraq, the United Nations, and its allies. Parents, for example, lose patience with the games played by children. The metaphor also trivializes the possibility of conflict. Losing patience hardly seems important in a prelude to war.

Making the Case / Selling the Plan

The final dominant metaphor in *NBC Nightly News* coverage of the prelude to war with Iraq depicted the Bush administration *making the case* for war, or, in another variation, *selling the plan*. A *case* can mean providing facts or evidence in support of a claim for law or a product. In this metaphor, the administration and its spokespersons were portrayed either as prosecutors presenting a case against a defendant or as salespeople trying to sell a product: war.

This metaphor was apparent in reporting on Secretary of State Colin Powell's February 5 presentation to the United Nations. That night, *NBC Nightly News* said Powell "spelled out with visual aids and *a prosecutor's rhetoric the administration's case* against Saddam Hussein." Another report, an interview with a former weapons inspector, said, "*His case was devastating.*" And later: "I think that *the case that* [sic] *was made* and was compelling," with "almost all, Republicans and Democrats, praising *the strength of Powell's case.*" That same day, the report said of the president and secretary of state, "The two men *tried to build a case* of Iraq's deception and denial." The *case* metaphor was used often throughout the time period studied. On March 5, the newscast began, "Countdown Iraq: The secretary of state *makes the strongest case* yet for war." The report said of Powell that, "today, he *marshaled the administration's case* against Saddam."

Making the case eventually also became *selling the plan*. The lexical change was significant. The administration figures were no longer prosecutors marshaling facts and pressing a case against defendants. They were salespeople "pitching" an idea, selling a plan. On February 6, the newscast described Bush and Powell: "First team. The president and Colin Powell, side by side, *selling the case* on Iraq." On February 14, a report said, "*Attempting to sell the war* at home, Mr. Bush argued again today that any battle against terror must include Iraq." The February 12 newscast said, "While Bush administration officials are convinced this latest bin Laden tape is proof of Iraq's ties to terrorists, it's *a hard sell* to the rest of the world." On February 26, the newscast began, "Target Iraq: President Bush talks about Iraq after a war, part of the administration's final *campaign to sell the plan.*"

Making the case and *selling the plan* borrow language from law, business, and marketing to offer portrayals of the weeks before war. *Making the case* proposes an interesting metaphor: Is the United States the prosecutor? Saddam Hussein the defendant? And who is the jury? The American people? The world? *Selling the plan* provides a more invidious perspective. No longer a time for the presentation of facts in a legal case, the weeks before war became a time for the huckster, the salesperson, making a pitch, hawking a product. And what is the product? "President Bush is *selling the war*."

METAPHORS CAN KILL

The subject of this detailed research is not the moral or political rightness or wrongness of the U.S. war with Iraq. The subject is the role of the news media, specifically in reporting the prelude to the 2003 invasion of Iraq. As a nation makes the decision to go to war, the news media should play a vital role. The news media can evaluate the rationales. They can verify claims. They can seek alternate views. They can weigh human and financial costs. They can assess outcomes. And they can provide a forum for debate.

The results of this study, while narrow in scope, suggest that the news media, at least the top-rated U.S. evening newscast, failed in these roles. *NBC Nightly News* did not provide a site in which the decision to go to war was in any way assessed, evaluated, or debated. In February and early March 2003, war was not inevitable. American allies worked furiously to forestall war. The UN Security Council refused to back the conflict. The UN secretary general and the pope both urged restraint. Millions protested for peace in the United States and around the world.

And yet, through metaphor, through the language of its newscasts, *NBC Nightly News* portrayed the United States as on a seemingly inevitable path to war. Rather than investigate, analyze, or debate the rationale for an unprovoked invasion, the broadcast instead offered, through metaphor, a dramatization of war unfolding. Accepting that the nation was on a *timetable*, dismissing inspections as the *games of Saddam*, giving voice to the frustration of the White House as it *lost patience* with the process, the broadcast then simply reported how the administration *made its case* and *sold its plan*.

NBC Nightly News was particularly interested, as you can see, in dramatizing and personalizing the process by which the nation, seemingly inevitably, entered into conflict. The network showed little interest in exploring calls for peaceful alternatives or evaluating the progress of inspections. It devoted little time or language to verifying claims, assessing evidence, establishing legalities, or weighing outcomes and aftermaths. Was Saddam a threat to the United States? Did Iraq have weapons of mass destruction? Was Saddam linked to terrorism, al-Qaeda, and Osama bin Laden? Was Saddam an impediment to Middle East peace? These questions went unasked by the broadcast.

Metaphor is a routine and unalterable aspect of human understanding. This critique has not questioned *NBC Nightly News* or other news outlets for employing metaphor in reporting the prelude to war with Iraq. It might as well question the newscast for using words. However, the metaphors used by *NBC Nightly News* displaced other possible metaphors that might have better profited a nation considering war. For example, the metaphor of a *claim* might have been a fruitful path to pursue. Through this metaphor, the Bush administration could have been understood as making particular *claims* about the regime of Saddam Hussein. Newscasts could have asked what evidence was introduced in support of those claims. Could the claims be verified? How did Saddam Hussein respond to those claims? How did other nations view the claims? The metaphor of the *claim*, as opposed to, for example, the *games of Saddam*, would have suggested more questioning and reporting by the news media. Another possible metaphor might have been a *debate*. The Bush administration could have been seen as engaging in a debate with Iraq, the United Nations, or its allies. What were its arguments in support of war? What were the counterarguments? Who made the counterarguments and to what effect?

Indeed, many other metaphors might have been employed. Metaphors of *negotiation*, of *process*, of *decision making*, and *deliberation* could have offered other directions. The purpose would have been to self-consciously employ language that invited debate, encouraged the investigation of claims, invited the assessment of outcomes, and ultimately fulfilled the essential role of the press for a nation considering war.

More than words were at stake. Lakoff and Johnson make clear that metaphors are linked to action:

> In most cases, what is at issue is not the truth or falsity of a metaphor but the perceptions and inferences that follow from it and the actions that are sanctioned by it. In all aspects of life, not just in politics or in love, we define our reality in terms of metaphors and then proceed to act on the basis of the metaphors. We draw inferences, set goals, make commitments, and execute plans, all on the basis of how we in part structure our experience, consciously and unconsciously, by means of metaphor.[30]

The Bush administration indeed took action and led the United States into war with Iraq. If a different system of metaphors had been used by U.S. news media, could war have been averted? The world will never know

Television viewers and media scholars may simply accept the vulgar promotion and anticipation of war as just another sign of the continued degradation of television news. This would be a mistake. Democratic debate is essential to civic life. Democratic debate about going to war is essential to global life. The news media have an indispensable, really irreplaceable, role in this process.

Professors and students have their own role as well. Scholarship, criticism, and interpretation can add to civic debates. The writer Susan Sontag argued that interpretation and criticism can rescue people from metaphors that kill. Interpretation and criticism, she said, are a means "to dissolve the metaphors" and a way to reveal "the unconscious system of metaphors that we use without awareness to comprehend reality."[31] Sontag argued that "the metaphors cannot be distanced just by abstaining from them. They have to be exposed, criticized, belabored, used up."[32] Through scholarship, discussion, and interpretation, the metaphoric language of television news can be "exposed, criticized, belabored, used up." The metaphors chosen can be identified and their implications made clear. And new metaphors—more thoughtful, encompassing, benign, or instructive—can be offered for use. Perhaps such attention to the language of the news media can help guard against metaphors that kill.

FACEBOOK REVOLUTION? MOHAMED BOUAZIZI

Mohamed Bouazizi was a twenty-six-year-old street vendor in the small town of Sidi Bouzid, Tunisia, in northern Africa. He burned himself to death in a protest. The protest helped lead to the fall of Tunisia's dictator and sent shockwaves throughout Africa and the Middle East. How could this young man's protest have been so influential? A *New York Times* columnist called it a "Facebook revolution."[33] It was a revolution as well for media and political globalization.

Bouazizi was one of seven children. He sold fruits and vegetables from a cart to help support his family. On December 17, 2010, he paid the equivalent of two hundred dollars for produce and began selling his merchandise in the town center. What happened next is unclear. Some accounts said police confronted Bouazizi for selling without a permit. Some accounts said Bouazizi refused to pay the police a bribe. All accounts agree: Police confiscated his produce and threw aside his cart. A female officer berated him, slapped him in the face, and spat at him. Bouazizi's humiliation was particularly acute. In many Arab cultures, women are to be subservient to men.[34]

Bouazizi had been harassed by the police before. He had had enough and went to the town governor's office to complain. The governor would not see him. Further humiliated, Bouazizi returned with gasoline or some other flammable fluids. He doused himself and set himself afire in protest. He was taken by ambulance to the hospital where he lingered in critical condition.

His family was outraged. They too went to the governor's gates in protest but were not granted entrance. "Our family can accept anything but not humiliation," Bouazizi's sister told a reporter.[35] They organized more protests. Some of the protesters took photographs on their cell phones and placed them on Facebook pages. Videos were posted on YouTube. News spread rapidly, especially among young people, and the protests grew. Many people had been angry for years over the corruption and violence of the government's military and police. The president of Tunisia, Zine el-Abidine Ben Ali, was a dictator who had ruled for twenty-three years. The people lived in poverty while government officials lived in luxury.

Protests increased and crowds swelled. Police tried to quell the crowds but only further inflamed the people. Al-Jazeera, the Arab TV network, learned of events through Facebook. It broadcast news of the protest throughout Tunisia and the Arab world.[36] The president, Ben Ali, suddenly understood the gravity of the situation. He made three television addresses to the people. He visited Bouazizi in the hospital.

On January 4, 2011, Bouazizi died from his wounds. Ten days later, President Ben Ali fled Tunisia for Saudi Arabia. Like the *New York Times*, media around the world proclaimed the Facebook revolution. Al Jazeera commented,

> In light of the dramatic development of events, on a considerable scale, it has become evident that new media have been playing a key role this time around in keeping the momentum going, and bringing the voices of the disengaged Tunisian youth to the attention of world media, and hence to international public opinion. Mobile phones, blogs, YouTube, Facebook pages and Twitter feeds have become instrumental in mediating the live coverage of protests and speeches, as well as police brutality in dispersing demonstrations. The internet in this case has assumed the role of a very effective uncensored news agency from which every broadcaster and news corporation have been able to freely source newsfeeds, raw from the scene.[37]

Bouazizi, family, friends, and Facebook had not only ignited change in Tunisia. Coverage of the dictator's overthrow had been seen throughout the Arab world. Protests erupted in Egypt. President Hosni Mubarak was driven from office. Uprisings occurred too in Yemen, Libya, and Syria. Were these truly "Facebook revolutions"?

NEW MEDIA IN THE GLOBAL VILLAGE

Thus far, we have looked closely at the role of traditional media in political globalization. However, our era has seen explosive growth and development in new media—media based on digital technology. Just a few decades ago, "new media" were technologies such as fax machines, audiocassettes, and VCRs. And all of these media made their mark on politics. One well-known example was the use of audiocassettes to spread the sermons of the exiled Ayatollah Khomeini in Iran in the 1970s. Eventually the Ayatollah built a base of support and led the Islamic Revolution, which still controls Iran.

Today, however, new media most often refer to digital technologies, such as computers, tablets, and cell phones. People increasingly communicate, collaborate, and get information and news through these devices.[38] In the context of political globalization, many people hope that new media and digital technology can improve politics in the global village.[39] They look at events in Tunisia, Egypt, and elsewhere and feel new media can allow alternative voices within and across borders. They hope new media will enlarge the public sphere. They feel new media can offer the opportunity for more people to be involved with political action and civil society.

And these new media do indeed have characteristics—mobile, interactive, discursive, and participatory—with dramatic political implications. Because of the low cost and ease of posting text, photos, video, music, and other material online, digital media allow for the possibility of multiple, varied voices and views that can challenge and question those in power. Citizens worldwide can post photos and dispatches from breaking news events via cell phones, computers, and webcams. Activists from around the globe can exchange information online and coordinate plans, demonstrations, and protests. Bloggers and online newspapers can find new outlets and audiences to challenge government and authority.

For example, the most read blog in the world each day is often beppegrillo.it.[40] The blog is published by the Italian comedian Beppe Grillo, who savagely satires Italian and European politics. Grillo regularly rails against corruption and scandal in his country and the European Union. He keeps a running list of Italian officials convicted of crimes. He has a "map of power" of the Italian stock exchange. He calls the Italian leader, Silvio Berlusconi, "Psychodwarf" and said of another Italian official, "In another country, he would have been the dishwasher in a pizzeria."[41] Such biting commentary could never appear in mainstream Italian media, which must be mindful of the power of politicians.

Iran also provides another good example of the increased role of new media in politics. Protests against a disputed presidential election in 2009 were met with brutal force. A twenty-six-year-old woman, Neda Agha-Soltan, was shot through the heart by a sniper. Graphic video and photos of the young woman dying were taken by cell phones and posted on Facebook, linked to Twitter, and widely circulated around the world within hours. "Neda" became a powerful symbol for the prodemocracy protesters, and her death increased international pressure on Iran. The Iranian protests became known as the "Twitter revolution."[42]

New media do indeed complicate politics. Yet, too often in discussions of political globalization and media, the promise of new media is overstated. I say this because new media voices can all too easily be silenced. In Egypt, for example, the government owns the Internet service provider, Telecom Egypt. During the 2011 revolt, the government simply shut down the Internet to prevent organizing through Facebook and other social media. New media can also be silenced in more primitive ways—by threatening people, by arresting them, and by killing them. Iran's Twitter revolution, for example, shows the limits of media power. The revolution ultimately was unsuccessful. Through a vicious crackdown, Iranian rulers further solidified their authority. And the government then used Facebook and other social media to track down and arrest protest leaders. In China, more than fifty thousand "cyberpolice" stalk the Internet usage of the Chinese people.[43]

Thus, people using new media can face the same harassment, intimidation, and persecution as traditional journalists. I will next tell the story of Raja Petra Kamarudin, Malaysia's most prominent blogger. Against all odds, he has succeeded in establishing a truly scathing, satirical political blog in a conservative Muslim majority nation. Raja Petra can serve as an exemplar of those around the world who continue to work in new media despite intense political pressure. His work shows the political possibilities—and the obstacles—facing new media in the global village. Though sometimes slow at first to recognize the possibility—and threat—posed by new media, established political and economic forces have moved quickly to assert control. Globalization complicates but does not lessen political intimidation and control of media in the global village. But Raja Petra is still alive. So let me tell you how extraordinary is the case of Raja Petra.

NEW MEDIA, MALAYSIA, AND THE CASE OF RAJA PETRA

I went to Malaysia a few years ago on a trip that started out as a university initiative at global outreach; I direct a program for research and study of globalization at Lehigh University, and we were making connections with universities, corporations, foundations, alumni, and future undergraduates. But wherever we went, when people found out I was also a professor of journalism, they wanted to talk about Raja Petra Kamarudin and his blog, *Malaysia Today*.

Some background is necessary. Just south of Thailand and north of Singapore, Malaysia is a relatively stable constitutional monarchy, an Asian democracy that has been under the control of one coalition government since the country's independence from Britain in 1957. The ethnic and religious mix in Malaysia is one of its most intriguing features. The Malay natives—the Bumiputera or Bumiputra, "Sons of the Soil"—make up 60 percent of the population and are overwhelmingly Muslim. However, 30 percent of the population are Chinese and 10 percent Indian—groups who were brought to Malaysia as laborers by Britain. Because of the dominant Muslim population, Malaysia is most often considered a secular Islamic state. Islam is the state religion but not the law of the land.[44]

The government, since independence from Britain, has been quite conservative. It does not allow much dissent and has kept tight control over the media. Though the Malaysian constitution guarantees freedom of speech, media control in Malaysia is older than the nation itself. Two censorship tools created by Britain in the 1940s—the Sedition Act and the Internal Security Act—were retained. The Internal Security Act allows for the arbitrary arrest of anyone who has committed—or is likely to commit—an act that is considered dangerous to "national security."[45]

More restrictions were put in place in the 1970s. Malaysia prides itself on its multiple cultures, but racial tensions simmer in Malaysia among the Malays, Chinese, and Indians. Race riots tore through Kuala Lumpur, the capital, in the 1970s. More than two hundred people, possibly many more, were killed. A state of emergency was declared, and the government suspended publication of all newspapers for days, claiming the papers spread ethnic hatred.[46] In the weeks after, the media were suppressed even more. There are now licensing acts for newspapers, magazines, and broadcast stations—licenses that must be renewed annually by the government. Finally,

Malaysian media are controlled by another basic means. Many media outlets are now owned or controlled by politicians or political parties.[47]

Under such political and religious restraints, self-censorship by the media has been more common than direct censorship and repression. Mainstream Malaysian media most often are seen as muted and meek.[48] Two scholars of the area write, "By and large and for a long, long time now, the Malaysian mainstream media have never aspired to be the guardians of freedom of speech.Very few would argue with the observation that, thus far, the mainstream Malaysian media have been nothing more than government mouthpieces."[49]

Given these conditions, you would think that the arrival of new media in Malaysia surely was met by immediate restrictions. The reality, surprisingly, is no. New media came to Malaysia in the 1990s in the latter half of the twenty-two-year rule of Prime Minister Mahathir Mohamad, who was in power from 1981 to 2003. Mahathir wanted Malaysia to become more advanced. He wanted the country to be one of Asia's "economic tigers." He had ambitious plans to create a Multimedia Super Corridor, a kind of Malaysian Silicon Valley, with satellite systems, digital television production, Internet services, research think tanks, and more. It was going to be almost three hundred square miles, stretching from the Petronas Twin Towers in downtown Kuala Lumpur to the KL Airport.[50]

However, to fulfill his plans, the prime minister needed small, innovative multimedia companies; large transnational corporations; foreign research and development centers; universities; and others—all of whom depended on the free flow of information. In a perhaps fateful decision, he promised that the Internet and other new media would not be licensed or censored, and this was encoded into law in 1998.[51]

Sex, Lies, and Websites

Events suddenly got wilder. Also in 1998, Mahathir suddenly fired his second in command, Deputy Prime Minister Anwar Ibrahim, and charged him with corruption and sodomy with a male aide. Anwar was arrested. The charge of sodomy was especially pertinent because it violated not only state law but was also an offense against Islamic law. Anwar had been a former Muslim youth leader who had been brought into the government to bolster the prime minister's standing among more conservative Muslims. But the two leaders disagreed often, and Anwar was emerging as a political rival. The charges against him seemed like a dramatic political ploy. Courts quickly found Anwar guilty, and he was imprisoned in September 1998.

Mainstream media, under the repressive regime, faithfully reproduced the prime minister's version of events and portrayed Anwar as guilty of the charges. There were some protests in the streets, but the demonstrations were broken up by police. Things might have stopped there.

But 1998, as you recall, was also the year of the new freedoms for the Internet. In a startling development for Malaysia, opposition emerged online. Websites were created specifically for Anwar's case, such as *Free Anwar*, *Justice for Anwar*, and *Voice of Freedom*. One observer at the time counted at least sixty sites.[52] The sites presented dramatically alternative views to the government and mainstream media. Much of the commentary was directed at Mahathir. He was called a rogue and a criminal by some of the online writers.[53] This opposition was a real test for Mahathir, who never before had to tolerate such public criticism. However, foreign companies, foundations, and universities were following events closely. Would the Internet remain free? In an extraordinary decision, Mahathir let the websites continue.

Many of the websites were short-lived. Anwar was serving his time in solitary confinement, and there was little to add. But the early sites set the foundation for a thriving online community in Malaysia. For example, *Malaysiakini* (Malaysia Now) was started in 1999 by two former print journalists and still survives as an online newspaper. Its content is quite different from the mainstream media.

And then we have Raja Petra Kamarudin, who had started not a newspaper but a blog, *Malaysia Today*, of biting political satire and commentary. And since 2004, Raja Petra has been the most popular blogger/columnist in Malaysia, regularly publishing columns with searing criticism of the government.[54]

The Crackdown

Perhaps Mahathir eventually got weary and wary of the criticism or felt that he had attracted enough foreign investors to his super corridor, but the inevitable crackdown came. In 2003, *Malaysiakini*, the online newspaper, had its offices raided and computers confiscated. A blogger, Jeff Ooi, was detained by police.[55] In both cases, Mahathir relied on religion, not politics, to justify his actions. The online sites, he said, were investigated for having insulted Islam. Raja Petra—perhaps because his focus was almost always political criticism or perhaps because of his huge popularity—went untouched by Mahathir. But a message had been sent by the government: the freedom of new media would now be limited.

Mahathir retired, and a succession of prime ministers replaced him. And they have proved more willing to crack down on new media.

In September 2008, Raja Petra was arrested on charges of publishing seditious—and anti-Islamic—articles. All of the nation's nineteen Internet service providers were commanded to prevent access to his website, including previous columns that had been allowed by Mahathir.[56]

Raja Petra recognized how religion and politics were joined to arrest him. He was willing to argue on those terms. He told the Committee to Protect Journalists, "I've been charged with everything, from insulting Islam, the prime minister, the sultans—every known living thing. But Islam makes it mandatory to oppose oppression. It's your duty, and it's what I'm doing."[57]

Maybe there was enough public and international outcry, or maybe the government just wanted to make a point, but Raja Petra was jailed for only two months. He was freed in early 1999. If the Malaysian government thought it had frightened him, it was mistaken. Raja Petra returned with fervor to his critical commentary.

Events then took another bizarre turn. You remember Anwar, the former deputy prime minister who was convicted of sodomy. Having served six years in prison, mostly in solitary confinement, he was released in 2004 and immediately again became an important oppositional political figure. He was working to build a coalition among Malaysia's ethnic groups. Then, in 2009, he was arrested, for a second time, on allegations of sodomy. Again, many claimed that the arrest was a political ploy. Charges and countercharges swirl around this latest trial, which continues to this day.[58]

And Raja Petra? He too was arrested again. The charges: sedition and insulting Islam. This time, however, Raja Petra feared things were going to be different for him. With a different, more repressive government in place, he might be going to jail for a long time. While awaiting trial, he fled the country. He now lives in exile in London, continuing to write his blog and speak out against censorship. He has not been tamed, and his incendiary pieces against the Malaysian government are read throughout Malaysia and the world.[59]

What are we to conclude from the case of Raja Petra? New media do offer the possibility of alternative political voices. Websites, blogs, Twitter, Facebook, and other tools still to come will continue to provide challenges to government and authority worldwide. But the stakes are high, and many forces can be brought to bear against those in new media. Access can be blocked. Costs can become prohibitive. Lawsuits can be brought. Arrests can be made. And, more directly, those in new media can be brutally silenced. The Committee to Protect Journalists has found that online journalists make up an increasing number of the journalists murdered worldwide.[60]

I have been emphatic throughout this book that the media are often complicit in the inadequacies and injustices of globalization. And we have seen in this chapter that the media have indeed contributed to the misery spawned by political globalization. Yet we have also seen that some journalists and others working in new media act heroically, courageously, in attempts to serve their society and fellow citizens. Our emphasis on human action and agency allows us to acknowledge the frailty—and nobility—of the human spirit.

On a concluding note, for twenty-two years, Malaysian prime minister Mahathir was the most powerful person in his nation, putting in place his economic reforms, creating the Multimedia Super Corridor, intimidating dissent, and keeping tight control on the mass media, including ultimately Raja Petra. Mahathir left the ruling party to handpicked successors. In recent years, however, his successors and the ruling party have veered from directions he set. His attempts to communicate with party leaders and redirect policy have been rebuffed. The media, following the lead of the ruling party, denies him access. Mahathir, though, has found a way to get his views back into Malaysia's public sphere. He started a blog.

7

MEDIA AND CULTURAL GLOBALIZATION

Cartoon Riots and Dismantled McDonald's

"THOSE DANISH CARTOONS"

In Libya, eleven people died in violent protests. In Beirut, close to three-quarters of a million people marched in the streets and set government offices and buildings aflame. Sixteen people were killed in northern Nigeria; less than a week later, another eight died. In Iran, embassies were attacked and burned.

The target of these demonstrations: newspaper cartoons.

The drawings—editorial cartoons of the Prophet Muhammad—were originally published in a small newspaper in Denmark. They ultimately led to worldwide riots, millions of dollars of damage, and more than a hundred deaths. The global outrage at the cartoons and the reaction to that outrage are stunning reminders of the complexities of media and culture in the global village.[1]

The media, on one level, are the primary carriers of culture. Through newspapers, magazines, movies, advertisements, television, radio, the Internet, and other forms, the media produce and display cultural products, from pop songs to top films. They also generate numerous and ongoing interactions among cultures, such as when American hip-hop music is heard by Cuban youth. Yet, with our emphasis on human action and agency, we know that the media are much more than technology, more than mechanical conveyors of culture, more than simple carriers of editorial cartoons or McDonald's advertisements. The media are people. These people are active economic agents and aggressive political lobbyists on matters of culture. They market brands aggressively. They seek out new markets worldwide for their cultural products. They actively bring about interactions of culture for beauty, power, and profit.

In some ways, these interactions are like cultural laboratory experiments. They sometimes result in startling and stunning hybrid creations. But other times they result in combustible and explosive mixtures. This chapter will offer a way to talk about and understand the varied outcomes that can come from the commingling of media, culture, and globalization. We will see that scholars try to capture this process in a number of conflicting theories. Some say that cultural contact will highlight differences and bring about a clash of civilizations. Others say that the cultural products of developed countries will overwhelm less developed cultures and lead to a homogenized world. Still others say that the mixture of cultures will result in new hybrid formations. I am skeptical of all-encompassing theories. In a global village of Babel, myriad interactions of culture are likely.

To extend a thought from the cultural anthropologist Arjun Appadurai, media are *global facts* that take *local form*.[2] The media and globalization are facts of life in local cultures. But local culture, I feel, is not static and fixed. Local culture is not pliable and weak, awaiting or fearing contact from the outside. Local culture is instead created and produced daily, drawing from, adopting, adapting, succumbing to, satirizing, rejecting, or otherwise negotiating with the facts, global and local, of the day. The local is built and understood anew each day in a globalized world.

The newspaper cartoons are a good place to start exploring all this. Sometimes lost in the fevered reporting of the cartoons was a simple realization. Prior to our era of globalization, editorial cartoons in Copenhagen likely would have had an impact *only in Copenhagen*. The interplay of globalization and media has brought people and cultures into closer contact than ever before. This is what we mean when we say globalization has compressed space and time. In our intensely interconnected world, space is overcome, and lines between local and global culture are blurred. Time, too, is overcome. Communication is instantaneous—and also long enduring. Originally published in September 2005, the cartoons caused immediate repercussions, repercussions that actually increased for months after and that continue to this day.

Indeed, the cartoons remain a sensitive and sore subject throughout the world. In 2010, a man attempted to kill one of the cartoonists but was shot by police.[3] The creators of the television cartoon *South Park* were threatened with death for a satirical episode that depicted Muhammad, an episode eventually censored by Comedy Central.[4] Cartoons, television shows, music, movies, plays, books, and more—media and globalization will continue to embroil, but also perhaps enrich, culture in our time.

LOCAL CARTOONS, GLOBAL RIOTS

It started with a simple news story. Early in September 2005, a leading newspaper in Denmark, *Politiken*, published an article about an author who was having trouble finding an illustrator for his children's book on Muhammad. Illustrators were afraid of the wrath of Muslims, the newspaper reported. Islamic tradition holds that visual images of Muhammad are forbidden.[5]

The story sparked debates in the country over self-censorship and intimidation. On September 30, 2005, another Danish newspaper, *Jyllands-Posten* (Jutland Post) published twelve editorial cartoons. Some of the cartoons attacked self-censorship. Some offered caricatures of Muhammad. An explanatory note by editor Flemming Rose said the cartoons were published to contest and reject the notion of possible censorship imposed by Muslims and to promote freedom of speech.[6]

Muslims in Denmark are a minority. They felt unjustly persecuted by the newspaper. No one among them had threatened a cartoonist. Why attack their religious beliefs in this way? they asked. Some of the cartoons seemed purposefully antagonistic. One, for example, showed Muhammad with a bomb in his turban. Another showed Muhammad greeting suicide bombers in heaven. Danish Muslims immediately protested to the paper. In mid-October, five thousand people marched peacefully outside the *Jyllands-Posten* office in Copenhagen.[7]

The local debate, however, was quickly becoming global. News spreads fast in a global village. Muslims worldwide were hearing about the cartoons. Five days after the march in Copenhagen, ambassadors from ten Muslim countries asked to meet with the prime minister of Denmark. He refused. He wanted, he said, to support freedom of speech. Over the next five months, the controversy smoldered. Muslim groups in numerous countries protested outside Danish embassies.[8]

Newspapers around the world began reporting on events. Some republished the cartoons, saying the republishing was necessary for an understanding of the story. Others said they republished the cartoons because they wanted to support freedom of speech. The republishing led to further protests. The governments of Pakistan, Saudi Arabia, Libya, Syria, and others condemned the cartoons. Boycotts of Danish goods were begun. Danes were threatened in many countries. More newspapers and some television stations—from India to New Zealand to Costa Rica to South Korea—showed the cartoons and editorialized against intimidation and censorship.[9]

The smoldering fire exploded. Throughout January and February 2006, violent demonstrations against the cartoons took place around the world. Embassies were attacked and burned. To get a sense of the global nature of the outrage, few countries did *not* see some form of protest. People were killed in Afghanistan, Somalia, Lebanon, Nigeria, Libya, and Pakistan. In all, more than one hundred people died.[10]

Though the violence had subsided by mid-2006, the issues saw no real resolution. As noted, death threats against the Danish cartoonists and others continue to this day. On one level, the issues are narrowly limited to a conflict between Islamic traditions and traditions of freedom of speech and the press. On a broader level, however, the issues transcend any one religion, group, or belief system. In a global village, all cultures will be coming into contact with increasing regularity. Traditions and values will be contested. Muslim women wear traditional Muslim dress in France, and French lawmakers protest. American films dominate the box offices of many nations that want to protect their own film industries. McDonald's restaurants are ubiquitous in many countries that want to protect their own restaurants and cuisine. What can we expect as cultures commingle and the global intrudes upon the local?

GLOBALIZATION AND CULTURE: THREE POSSIBLE OUTCOMES

In his wise book, *Globalization and Culture: Global Mélange*, Jan Nederveen Pieterse argues that there are actually three, and only three, outcomes with which to consider the influence of globalization on culture.[11]

Cultural differentialism suggests that cultures are different, strong, and resilient. Distinctive cultures will endure, this outcome suggests, despite globalization and the global reach of American or Western cultural forms. For some, this outcome is ominous for our era of globalization. It suggests that cultures are destined to clash as globalization continually brings them together. The Danish cartoon controversy might be understood under this outcome.

Cultural convergence suggests that globalization will bring about a growing sameness of cultures. A global culture, likely American culture, some fear, will overtake many local cultures, which will lose their distinctive characteristics. For some, this outcome can suggest "cultural imperialism," in which the cultures of more developed nations "invade" and take over the cultures of less developed nations. The result will be a worldwide, homogenized, Westernized culture.

Cultural hybridity suggests that globalization will bring about an increasing blending or mixture of cultures. This mélange will lead to the creation of new and surprising cultural forms, from music to food to fashion. For Pieterse—the subtitle of his book is *Global Mélange*, you recall—this outcome is common, occurs throughout history, and will occur more so in an era of globalization.

The three outcomes do a splendid job of organizing what could be thousands of distinct examples of the meeting of global and local culture. My own preference is not to give preference or privilege to any one theory. No one outcome or paradigm is "right." Or, rather, they are all "right"— sometimes. By placing the three outcomes on a continuum, with no stark divisions, Pieterse's trio allows us to locate specific, historically situated meetings of global and local forms at one point, or maybe even multiple points, on the continuum.

cultural differentialism ↔ cultural hybridity ↔ cultural convergence

With this crude continuum in mind, we can organize some of the most vexing issues, theories, and events within the realm of media, culture, and globalization. As we saw, the violence surrounding the Danish editorial cartoons can likely be placed fairly far to the left of the continuum for cultural differentialism. The disappearance of hundreds of languages, as a few languages become dominant, can be placed far right on the continuum for cultural convergence. Jazz is an archetypal example of cultural hybridity and would sit comfortably in the middle of the continuum.

In the next sections, I hope to show how each of these outcomes is evident, even prevalent, in our world, and in surprising ways. To demonstrate this, I will show how McDonald's—the ubiquitous American restaurant chain—actually can be found representing each of the three outcomes on the continuum. The Golden Arches, along with other examples, will show the complexity of culture in the global village. And because culture is most often *mediated*, we will see how media complicate and enrich cultural globalization.

CULTURAL DIFFERENCE: MCDONALD'S AND "THE CLASH OF CIVILIZATIONS?"

In 1999, José Bové catapulted to worldwide fame. He destroyed a McDonald's.

Bové was a French farmer and social activist. He was particularly interested in politics and agriculture. He led campaigns to protect sheep farmers in France, to promote organic gardening, and to advocate for other causes. He then became involved in protests against hormone-treated beef. He became incensed when he learned that McDonald's, one of the largest buyers of meat in the world, used hormone-treated beef. Bové was also concerned about the influence of McDonald's on French food and life. To draw attention to the issues, he called media outlets and told them he would lead an attack on a new McDonald's restaurant in Millau, a town in southern France. Days before the restaurant opened, Bové's group literally took the restaurant apart and dumped the rubble outside the town hall.[12]

Bové was a master of media manipulation. The publicity stunt succeeded far beyond his expectations. The protest was reported worldwide. Though he was imprisoned for forty-four days, Bové became an international celebrity and spokesperson. Perhaps just as significant, he established McDonald's as a symbolic target for those concerned about global issues, from food to the environment to labor to globalization itself. Protests against McDonald's continue to be part of antiglobalization or alter-globalization demonstrations. The shattered glass of a McDonald's restaurant window has become emblematic of such protests around the world.

The protests certainly represent one end of our continuum. As we have seen, the outcome of cultural difference suggests that cultures are strong and that distinctive cultures will fight to retain their differences, despite globalization. The smashing of a McDonald's represents cultural difference as local cultures attempt to resist the culinary practices and eating habits fomented by this icon of America. Some scholars take this concept further. They suggest that, because cultures will remain different, they are ordained to clash as globalization brings them closer together. This view has immense implications for how one understands the world today, and I want to spend some time with the argument.

In 1993, the late Harvard political scientist Samuel Huntington published a controversial but ultimately hugely influential paper titled "The Clash of Civilizations?" He offers a bleak view of globalization and culture in our time:

> It is my hypothesis that the fundamental source of conflict in this new world will not be primarily ideological or primarily economic. The great divisions among humankind and the dominating source of conflict will be cultural. Nation states will remain the most powerful actors in world affairs, but the principal conflicts of global politics will occur between nations and groups of different civilizations. The clash of civilizations will dominate global politics. The fault lines between civilizations will be the battle lines of the future.[13]

The article identifies seven civilizations—"Western, Confucian, Japanese, Islamic, Hindu, Slavic-Orthodox, Latin American and possibly African."[14] But as a U.S. professor and policy maker, Huntington has one particular concern in mind: "The West versus the Rest." He argues that the spread of Western values and beliefs in a globalized world will antagonize and provoke other cultures. And as those cultures attempt to assert or protect themselves, conflict will be a natural result. His most pointed arguments concern Islamic culture, which he sees as an aggressive challenger to the West. "Islam," he says in a startling phrase, "has bloody borders."[15] Huntington concludes his piece with policy suggestions based on enhancing dominance of the West while weakening "the Rest." His thoughts include limiting the military strength of Confucian and Islamic states, maintaining Western military superiority in East and Southwest Asia, exploiting differences and conflicts among Confucian and Islamic states, and supporting groups that might be sympathetic to the West.[16]

The article attracted much attention—positive and negative—and in 1996 Huntington published a book on the topic. Five years after the book's publication, on September 11, 2001, when the United States was attacked by Islamic militants, the "clash of civilizations" received renewed interest. Huntington's thesis, to some, seemed prophetic. Publications worldwide revisited its claims. For example, the *New York Times* published an interview with Huntington the following month headlined "A Head-On Collision of Alien Cultures?"[17]

But are the United States and the West indeed doomed to a head-on collision with Islam? Is the fruit of media, culture, and globalization to be disharmony and discord? Pieterse and other scholars do not think so. In fact, Huntington's work has been savaged by many in the academic community. They decry its simplistic representation of civilizations and its militaristic posture.

Pieterse, for example, derides Huntington's "crude rendition" of civilizations as geographical entities, "tectonic plates" at whose fault lines conflict is likely.[18] He charges too that "Huntington recycles the Cold War." For Huntington, Pieterse says, "the Cold War is over but war is everlasting."[19] Appadurai says of Huntington's thesis, "In a word, it evacuates history from culture, leaving only geography. The world appears as a large series of slowly moving cultural glaciers."[20] Similarly, Edward Said, in an essay titled "The Clash of Ignorance," finds that Huntington ignores the varied dynamics and pluralities *within* every civilization. Said argues that "the personification of enormous entities called 'the West' and 'Islam' is recklessly affirmed, as if hugely complicated matters like identity and culture existed in a cartoonlike world where Popeye and Bluto bash each other mercilessly."[21]

Despite sharing these strong rejections of Huntington's thesis, I continue to have students in my classes read "The Clash of Civilizations?" and wanted to review its argument here because the media are deeply implicated. How do people learn to hate others whom they have never met? How do they derive stereotyped distortions of other religions and races? How do political leaders stoke followers to become blood-foamed killers who carry out ethnic cleansing? Often, the media are active participants.

For example, in 1994, more than eight hundred thousand people—perhaps one million—were slaughtered in the East African nation of Rwanda. On one level, the horror showed the inadequacy of Huntington's work; what happened in Rwanda was a campaign of ethnic violence by the majority Hutu population against the minority Tutsi. On another level, the horror showed the complicity of media in cultural globalization. In *The Media and the Rwanda Genocide*, scholars paint a devastating portrait of local newspapers and radio stations fueling the slaughter.[22] The local media spread fear, reported rumors, incited violence, and even gave instructions on carrying out the massacre. Most international news media ignored the genocide, unaware of, or uninterested in, the catastrophe. The few Western reports that made note of events misunderstood their severity. Though the Rwanda massacre was extreme, around the world, by omission or commission, by careless language or stereotyped frames, media add to the divides between peoples and cultures.

What are we to make of all this? No doubt, globalization will increasingly bring cultures and people together. And cultures will sometimes clash. Local forces will try to protect their traditions. The global village can have contentious corners. However, is that the destiny of humankind? Others argue that the commingling of cultures can bring about very different results.

CULTURAL CONVERGENCE: MCDONALDIZATION OR MCWORLD?

In Malaysia's Kuala Lumpur, I am walking along a main thoroughfare, Jalan Bukit Bintang, in the heart of the city. The street is quintessentially Malaysian—with storefronts and restaurants displaying the country's rich mixture of Malay, Chinese, and Indian cultures. Women pass in burqas and chadors—Malays are predominantly Muslim. At an outdoor restaurant, a young couple passes a hookah back and forth. The acrid tobacco smell drifts across the sidewalk. I turn a corner and the Bukit Bintang monorail is overhead. Beneath the monorail, at a busy intersection packed with pedestrians, cars, trucks, and buses, I find—Ronald McDonald sitting on a bench outside a McDonald's restaurant.

It is actually a statue of Ronald, big, bright, yellow, and red. Despite the bustle of the intersection, the gaudy statue sticks out. A steady stream of people flows in and out of the restaurant. I venture inside. I ask and get permission to take photos. One of my favorites is a striking Muslim woman in a black chador thoughtfully eating her Big Mac.

Ray Kroc derived the name and the idea of fast, inexpensive, mass-produced food from two brothers—named McDonald, of course—who had a California hamburger stand. Kroc opened his first McDonald's in Des Plaines, Illinois, in 1955. And now McDonald's has more restaurants overseas than in America. The restaurants, arches, products, brands, and advertisements are seemingly everywhere. In fact, there are thirty-two thousand restaurants in 119 countries on six continents. They serve more than fifty-two million people every day.[23]

Though the destruction of McDonald's restaurants symbolizes the differences and clashes among cultures, the sheer ubiquity of McDonald's certainly can point to an opposing position—cultural convergence. As you recall, cultural convergence suggests that media and globalization will bring about a homogenization of cultures, and that Western culture, especially American culture, will overwhelm local traditions. Differences exist among McDonald's restaurants in various countries, and we will explore those differences in the next section. But the global reach and ever-present marketing of the American-based chain argues for cultural convergence—engulfing local culture not only with American cuisine, but with American production routines, habits, and tastes.

Sociologist George Ritzer coined the term *McDonaldization* to capture "the process by which the principles of the fast-food restaurant are coming to dominate more and more sectors of American society as well as of the rest of the world."[24] Those rational principles—such as efficiency, predictability, calculability, and control—now manifest themselves, Ritzer says, in education, work, criminal justice, health care, travel, religion, and almost every other area of life in America and around the globe.[25] And again we can see the media as integral to the process, transmitting, advertising, and celebrating American products and practices. Can we really say that media and globalization will bring about a McWorld? Some have.

"McWorld—Hey, It Could Happen!"

In the early 1990s, McDonald's ran a series of television advertisements during Saturday-morning cartoons. The ads offered fun fantasies of what might happen if children ran the world. The fantasies included no homework, gym class replacing traditional classes, and of course people eating McDonald's for every meal. Each of the ads ended with a shout— "McWorld! Hey, it could happen!"

In 1992, political scientist Benjamin Barber published an article in *The Atlantic*, "Jihad vs. McWorld."[26] Barber likely was not a viewer of Saturday-morning cartoons and was unaware of the McWorld ads. His version of McWorld, as you might expect, is strikingly different from McDonald's. Barber saw that globalization was changing our world. He was interested in what kind of world might result. His provocative opening paragraph offers two possible futures, both bleak.

The first future is marked by violent division, "in which culture is pitted against culture, people against people, tribe against tribe." He calls this Jihad. The second future is marked by stultifying sameness and conformity, by forces "that mesmerize the world with fast music, fast computers, and fast food" and lead to "one McWorld tied together by technology, ecology, communications, and commerce."[27] Barber subsequently published a book that extended the argument, also called *Jihad vs. McWorld*.[28]

In Pieterse's terms, *Jihad vs. McWorld* is cultural differentialism versus cultural convergence. Barber's work is appealing because, unlike other overarching theorists, Barber does not argue for one outcome over another. Indeed, he sees the world falling apart and coming together at the same time. Yet for Barber, like Ritzer, McDonald's is a homogenizing force. McWorld is cultural convergence. In an interview, Barber said,

> So here you had these two portraits of the world, one showing the world falling to pieces and the other saying it was coming together, and both of them seemed to me to be true, however contradictory. So I set out to write a book to try to map and explain a world in which both those statements could be true at the same time, and indeed were true in ways that related to one another and actually had something to do with some of the same forces. Obviously, I used jihad as a general rubric under which I could examine the zealous, anti-modern, disintegrative forces that were helping break the world into pieces, and I invented the term McWorld to refer to the axis of global communication and global pop culture, global technology and global trade around which the world was coming together.[29]

In his original article, Barber similarly describes McWorld as "the onrush of economic and ecological forces that demand integration and uniformity and that mesmerize the world with fast music, fast computers and fast food—with MTV, Macintosh and McDonald's, pressing nations together into one commercially homogenous global network."[30]

Media scholars have taken McDonald's and cultural convergence a step further. They have seen cultural convergence in terms of domination and control. The thesis of "cultural imperialism" is that dominant cultures, often exemplified by Western states and corporations, impose their culture, either directly or indirectly, on others for economic and political gain.[31] John Downing, Ali Mohammadi, and Annabelle Sreberny-Mohammadi point out that "imperialism is the conquest and control of one country by a more powerful one. *Cultural imperialism* signifies the dimensions of the process that go beyond economic exploitation or military force."[32] Such imperialism, they say, often takes place in the very fabric of some nations. The authors remind us that colonial powers established educational systems and media systems in many countries that exist to this day and reflect Western culture. Current media too, such as advertising, also reinforce Western culture. "Subtly but powerfully, the message has often been insinuated that Western cultures are superior," they say.[33] That is cultural imperialism.

For example, Ghana, once the site of a powerful African empire, was colonized by the British in the late 1800s and only achieved independence in 1957. The country still strives to secure and maintain its cultural traditions but has watched with dismay as young people have embraced the music and dress of the West, its former colonizers. Queen Nana Ama Ayensua Saara, of the Denkyira in Ghana, recently addressed a conference at the University of Ghana in Legon. The subject of her concern was the preservation of her country's cultural heritage and identity among youth in the face of globalization. The Ghana Broadcasting Corporation detailed her arguments:

> She said the forces of globalization and urbanization are fast eroding the country's cultural values even to the extent that many of the youth do not know their appellations and roots. She described as suicidal and unacceptable, the negative life style of the youth with respect to their mode of dressing. She said it is common to see young ladies wearing dresses and brassieres with 90 percent of their breast exposed, also exposed are their under pants and beads. She also expressed concern about the "Ottofister" style exhibited by boys by pulling down their trousers and exposing their pants and buttocks as completely at variance with the country's cultural values.[34]

Parents in the West, too, complain of such modes of dressing. The complaint, though, rises above taste and fashion and takes on more urgency and depth in the context of colonialism, globalization, and the possibility of cultural imperialism.

How do Western values and style infiltrate far-off nations such as Ghana? Through the media—through film, music videos, television, advertising, websites, and more. Indeed, the media's role is so fundamental to cultural imperialist theories that sometimes the process is called "media imperialism." UNESCO, you recall, was the site of impassioned debates over media imperialism in the 1970s and 1980s. Developing nations wanted to limit the access of large Western media to their peoples. They called for a New World Information and Communication Order (NWICO).[35] Western nations resisted such limitations and claimed they violated free speech. Ultimately, in 1984, the United States and the United Kingdom bitterly left UNESCO for almost twenty years, only rejoining when the issue was dropped.

Critics say the cultural imperialism or media imperialism thesis has a simplistic, even degrading view of developing countries' cultures as passive and weak. They say cultures are strong enough and resilient enough to adapt or reject Western culture.[36] Appadurai, for example, finds that the intersection of global and local cultures brings about "a space of contestation in which individuals and groups seek to annex the global into their own practices of the modern."[37] But the cultural imperialism thesis does touch upon the fear and anger felt by other countries and cultures as they try to resist cultural convergence and retain their autonomy in an era of globalization—and the omnipresence of McDonald's.

McDonald's as cultural convergence. McDonald's as cultural difference. Can we also see McDonald's in terms of cultural hybridity?

CULTURAL HYBRIDITY: MCCURRY AND GLOCALIZATION

Mumbai is a city of staggering contrasts. Large desperate slums seethe in the shadows of luxurious shopping malls and entertainment centers. The Phoenix Mills mall, a complex of converted former factories, is a huge, multistory shopping behemoth with numerous global brands, restaurants, and shops represented. It is at first not surprising to see a bustling McDonald's in Phoenix Mills, until you consider that Indians are predominantly Hindus. They feel that the cow is sacred and do not eat beef. But what is McDonald's without beef and burgers? Plenty.

Inside the McDonald's in Phoenix Mills—and in McDonald's across India—you will find, instead of a Big Mac, a Chicken Maharaja Mac. You will find vegetarian and nonvegetarian menus above the counter. Under

"Meal Combos," you will find McVeggie Burger with Cheese, McCurry Pan Shahi Paneer, McCurry Pan Shahi Chicken Paneer, Salsa Wrap, and more. In countries around the world, local McDonald's have adapted the global McDonald's brand to local customs. Japan has Ebi Chiki, shrimp nuggets; Ebi Filet-O, burgers made of shrimp; and Koroke burgers, made of potato, cabbage, and katsu sauce. Norway has McLaks—grilled salmon on a bun.

China, of course, is a huge market with almost a quarter of the world's population. McDonald's has adapted to Chinese culture as well.[38] *China Daily* noted the process approvingly. It wrote, "McDonald's Vegetable and Seafood Soup and Corn Soup were introduced, and the company worked to modify the restaurants' design. During the 2004 Spring Festival, McDonald's on Beijing's Wangfujing Street attracted many people with a traditional Chinese look, decorating their interiors with papercuts of the Chinese character Fu (Happiness), magpies and twin fishes, all auspicious symbols." The newspaper concluded, "Two cultures proactively crashed, connected, and assimilated."[39] Shannon Peters Talbott did an ethnographic study of McDonald's in Moscow and arrived at a similar conclusion: McDonald's represented the localization of the global.[40]

In Pieterse's terms, McDonald's has actively engaged in cultural hybridity, the blending and mixing of cultures. Certainly the hybrid McDonald's creations—McCurry Pan Shahi Paneer—are not done merely out of respect for other traditions. These are business decisions. Why open up a hamburger restaurant in a land where most people do not eat meat? And throughout history, we can see that business, religion, politics, leisure, labor, and more have brought cultures together and spawned new hybrid creations.

In that time, cultural hybridity has gone by many names—mixing, syncretism, creolization, mestizaje, and more. As globalization has increased the frequency of such contact and mixing, the world has been given another ugly, awkward term—*glocalization*. Its origins are murky; some say that Sony chairman Akio Morita coined the term.[41] Though I don't care for the word, *glocalization* does capture the essence of what we are discussing. The commingling of global and local is a process in which global facts take local form. Local life—everyday life in each nook and cranny of the global village—is active and fluid. By focusing on the interaction of local and global, we affirm that local cultures are not passive or helpless in the face of global culture.

Once again, we can see that media are essential. Sometimes the media can be sites of glocalization. For example, a Malaysian version of the hit television show *American Idol* is called *Imam Muda* (Young Leader). As in

American Idol, contestants appear before a panel of judges. But the winner does not receive a record contract but a position as a fledgling imam, or religious leader, a scholarship to study in Saudi Arabia and a pilgrimage to Mecca.[42] The global has taken local form. Other times, the media are agents of glocalization. Cuban youths excitedly listened to black popular music from Miami radio and television shows during the 1970s, later learned of the emerging rap and hip hop scene, and eventually developed their own style of Cuban hip hop.[43] In and through media, from music to video games to film to advertising and more, local people adapt global culture to everyday life. Music especially has been a site for cultural hybridity. The next section looks at a lovely example.

CULTURAL HYBRIDITY AND MUSIC: OMARA PORTUONDO AND CUBAN *FILIN*

The film catches a powerful moment. Two singers, skin burnished and brown as soft leather, with voices deepened by age and experience, are finishing a live performance of a tender, heartbreaking song, "Silencio." The woman sings to the man of her deep sorrow. She feels the need, she sings to her partner, to hide her great pain, even from her flowers, lest they wither under her torment.

> *No quiero que sepan mis penas*
> *porque si me ven llorando moriran.*
> I do not want you to know my pain
> because if you see me crying, you will die.

Even as the woman is finishing the song, her eyes brim with tears. Her partner sees her glistening cheeks as they bow together and instinctively uses his fingers to brush away the tears, tears caused by the beauty of their song.

The singers are Omara Portuondo and Ibrahim Ferrer, and the scene is from the 1999 film *Buena Vista Social Club*.[44] A legendary music club in Havana, Cuba, the Buena Vista Social Club helped make the city a cultural capital for music, cabaret, and dance during the 1940s, years before Castro and the revolution. In the 1990s, Cuban musicians, including some from the 1940s, joined with American guitarist and producer Ry Cooder to re-create the sounds of that era. The performances and soundtrack inspired the documentary film by Wim Wenders, which went on to receive an Academy Award nomination for Best Documentary Feature and to win Best Documentary at the European Film Awards. It also brought worldwide acclaim to many of the Cuban musicians, some in their nineties.

Though the film brought new audiences to her work, Omara Portuondo had already spent a lifetime moving comfortably between local and global music as well as local and global fame. Portuondo provides an insightful case of cultural hybridity and represents the ability of artists throughout the world to resist the dislocations of economic, political, and cultural globalization and instead to turn those dislocations into stirring works of imagination and beauty.

Portuondo's life represented hybridity from its roots.[45] Her mother, daughter of a wealthy Spanish family, fell in love and married a black Cuban baseball player. A product of the forbidden mixed marriage, Portuondo understood better than most the clash of cultures. Her mother and father could not talk, for example, if they passed on the streets of Havana.[46] Portuondo's talents as a singer and dancer were obvious at an early age, and as a teenager she served as a backup performer in Havana's glorious but notorious Tropicana cabaret, home to Latin American high rollers and American gangsters.[47]

Havana, with dance clubs and cabarets like the Tropicana and Buena Vista Social Club, was then a crossroads for big bands, artists, and performers, a crossroads of cultures. During off hours, Portuondo and friends traded songs and ideas, creating music that pulled from American jazz and Cuban bossa nova as well as Argentinean and Brazilian strains and African rhythms.[48] The hybrid sound spread through Havana and was given the name "feeling," or "*filin*" in Spanish. Portuondo was introduced as "the fiancée of feeling" and is still known by many Cubans as "la novia del filin."[49] The friends formed the Cuarteto Las D'Aida and quickly found artistic, commercial, and cultural success. They made an album for RCA Victor, toured America, performed with Nat King Cole, and introduced Cuban culture and their hybrid music form to the world.

On January 1, 1959, life in Cuba was irrevocably changed when the rebel forces of Fidel Castro overthrew the dictatorship of Fulgencio Batista and carried the communist revolution to power. For many artists, the revolution was a wrenching turning point. The revolution brought an end to the profligate nightlife of clubs, casinos, and cabarets. The government closed or took over the operations, including the Tropicana Club. Cuban artists, too, were placed under the control of the state. Many artists fled the country for Europe, Puerto Rico, Florida, or New York. Others who were touring the world did not come back.[50]

Portuondo was faced with a stark choice. Her first solo album came out in 1959—just as the revolution was taking control—and further established her reputation for blending Cuban music with the music of the world. She could have launched her career abroad. But Portuondo never deserted Cuba. She resisted the riches of exile and split life between the impoverished island and the performing arts centers of the world. She recalls times in Cuba when musicians were put to work in the sugarcane fields, singing to the workers as they harvested the crops.[51] "So many singers had gone into exile that there was a gap to be filled," she says.[52]

Decades later, the Buena Vista Social Club album and film introduced her to new audiences. Even in her seventies, Portuondo toured the world from Japan to Sweden. Her life and music exemplify the creative potential within globalization and media. Music, and perhaps art in general, from painting to film, show the possibilities and promise of cultural globalization. From American jazz to Cuban *filin* to Japanese rap to French bluegrass, music seems to relentlessly mix genres, styles, and cultures. Music seems to effortlessly blend the local and global. It would be wonderful to write that such creative hybrids will always be the outcome of the ongoing interactions of media, culture, and globalization. Yet, as this chapter has shown, three outcomes are possible, and only sometimes will hybridity be the case.

CULTURAL GLOBALIZATION AND CHINA: QIANGGUO LUNTAN AND TIANANMEN

"China Must Learn to Project Power," "Affordable Housing Tests Beijing's Mettle," "Chinese Millionaires and Their Bubbles"[53]—these essays are just some of the hundreds of postings to be found at Qiangguo Luntan (Strong Nation Forum or Strengthening Nation Forum) and other online chat rooms of China's *People's Daily*. The site pulses with political, economic, and cultural conversations. Such dialogue might be surprising to those with a one-dimensional view of Chinese media as a repressive, state-controlled system. I wanted to include in this chapter on cultural globalization a brief but important reference to Chinese media and culture. China shows how the processes of globalization—economic, political, and cultural—often intersect and intertwine in unpredictable ways.[54]

China's embrace of globalization has resulted in a delicately nuanced negotiation of the global and local. It is wonderfully complicated. Chinese leaders seek the benefits of commercial interactions with the West and economic globalization. Yet they also strive to promote and maintain local and national culture and to resist possible convergence with Western culture through cultural globalization. All the while, they endeavor to build China's global status and maintain local power and control in a time of political globalization. In effect, Chinese leaders have broken down globalization into its three processes and are choosing their preferred blend.

International communication scholars Paula Chakravartty and Yuezhi Zhao arrive at a similar point when they note that Chinese officials often avoid altogether using the broad term *globalization*. Officials instead opt for the more specific phrase, *economic globalization*. The emphasis, Chakravartty and Zhao say, signifies "the Chinese state's attempt to integrate with the global market system on the one hand, and resist political and cultural assimilation into the American-dominated global capitalist order on the other."[55] That is, China's approach has been to embrace economic globalization while attempting to manage and control cultural and political globalization. As Chakravartty and Zhao suggest, the situation is complicated even further: the balance between global and local is often distilled simply to the U.S.-China relationship. China participates in this era of globalization, but with a wary eye on the United States.

The wariness extends to surprising corners. For example, Liu Kang, another scholar of communication, culture, and China, finds that Chinese journalists balance desires for press freedom with a nationalism born of suspicion over U.S. attempts to promote such freedom. He writes,

> Hence it becomes imperative that understanding China's freedom of press, political reform, and nationalism must take into account the U.S.-China relationship as a central component of China's "domestic" issues. Nothing remains purely "internal affairs" in China without the "interferences" of influences of the United States.[56]

In the perspective of this chapter, Chinese nationalism can be partially understood as one aspect of people's negotiation of the global and local—or the U.S. and China—relationship. Postings at the *People's Daily* forum support this view. Writers often balance their questions and reproach of Chinese practices with critiques of the United States. For example, one essay critically appraised freedom for new media in China, but the writer also added, "While Hillary Clinton adds some $20 million to the already $25 million annual budget to force 'internet freedom' at other countries, their senators are fighting to reduce the national budget for education, health, R&D, and many more. They care more for countries like Syria, China, and Iran, than their own people."[57] We can find the balance of global and local culture even in a single online post. Things get more complicated when we consider Tiananmen Square.

"Tank Man," Tiananmen, and Media

You may recall the now-iconic news image from the June 1989 demonstrations in Beijing's Tiananmen Square. After weeks of huge protests in the square and then a military crackdown that killed hundreds of people, a lone man in a white shirt stepped into the square and stood defiantly in front of a column of tanks. Photographers shot the picture, and it appeared on the front pages of newspapers worldwide. The London newspaper the *Telegraph* ranked it among "ten photographs that changed the world"; *Time* magazine said the man "revived the world's image of courage."[58]

My university not long ago hosted a conference on culture, communication, and China. Two renowned scholars mentioned above, Yuezhi Zhao and Liu Kang, anchored the day. Amid the wide-ranging, daylong presentations, panel, and discussions, we often found ourselves returning to the image of the figure who has come to be known as "Tank Man." The picture is more than twenty years old. Our references to the photo suggest its enduring status. But it soon became clear that the image has more than historical interest. It has become an intriguing exemplar of negotiating global and local culture.

For many Americans and others in the West, "Tank Man" is a classic picture of a confrontation between democratic values and a repressive state. A lone individual, seeking freedom, bravely faces down a powerful symbol of state power—a column of tanks. The picture seems to represent humankind's desire for democracy and freedom, desires stifled by the Chinese authorities. Indeed, here is how a writer in the *New York Times* described the picture on its twentieth anniversary:

> Few images are more recognizable or more evocative. Known simply as "tank man," it is one of the most famous photographs in recent history. Twenty years ago, on June 5, 1989, following weeks of huge protests in Beijing and a crackdown that resulted in the deaths of hundreds, a lone man stepped in front of a column of tanks rumbling past Tiananmen Square. The moment instantly became a symbol of the protests as well as a symbol against oppression worldwide—an anonymous act of defiance seared into our collective consciousnesses.[59]

However, as our conference progressed, attendees learned that the photograph has a very different meaning for Chinese officials. The officials point to videos of the scene that apparently show the tanks *leaving* the square, the man stepping in front of them, and the tanks reversing, changing course, and trying to maneuver around the man. For Chinese leaders, the photograph is actually a symbol of the Chinese state's restraint and the measured actions of its military. From the perspective of the Chinese, the moment captured by the photographers is being deliberately misinterpreted at the global level as an attack on China. The image thus evokes contrary interpretations at the global and local level—a global fact that takes different, contradictory local forms. And, to add to the complexity, since the image remains subject to dispute, it is largely blocked on the Internet inside China and is thus actually unknown to many Chinese.

THE DAILY (AND HISTORICAL) NEGOTIATION
OF LOCAL AND GLOBAL

Of globalization's three processes—economic, political, and cultural—many people see cultural globalization as especially important in our era. They see riots over cartoons of Muhammad and demonstrations against immigrants. They see heightened security at airports over fear of "Islamic terrorists" and U.S. military action in Islamic nations. They see Western products adopted around the world and American flags burned in protest. They see fast-food restaurants in remote villages and McDonald's menus with McCurry and McLaks. They see the huge global box office of *Titanic* and the rise of Bollywood as a competitor to Hollywood.

Through a simple continuum, we have tried to organize outcomes for the seemingly infinite intersections of media, culture, and globalization. We have shown, for example, that McDonald's can be situated on all points of the continuum, that McDonald's can exemplify cultural differentialism, cultural convergence, and cultural hybridity, and that McDonald's, of all things, demonstrates that cultural globalization is a complex and multifarious process. We have seen that the commingling of cultures may lead to a clash of cultures, a homogenizing of cultures, and striking cultural creations. We have seen how essential the media are for all paradigms of cultural globalization.

Perhaps the larger lesson from all this is that no one theory can capture the varied interactions that occur when local culture comes into contact with other cultures. Even if we just consider two factors—media and migration—we can see that cultures are going to come into contact thousands of times a day in thousands of different ways. Media make available news, music, film, comedy, fashion, sports, and more, twenty-four hours a day, seven days a week. Migration, study abroad, tourism, business, and more bring people from other cultures into contact regularly. Contact between global and local culture is now the norm, not the exception.

Our very understanding of local culture actually benefits from the long, historical lens of globalization. Local culture is likely the historical product of countless previous interactions with other cultures. That is, local culture in our time is a product of negotiation between local and global cultures of previous times. Country to country, city to city, neighborhood to neighborhood, the negotiation of local culture and other cultures has taken place and will take place daily over time. Rather than being fixed and static, local culture is continually produced and reproduced every day.

This daily "negotiation" between local culture and other cultures is key to understanding globalization, media, and culture. The global village allows the intersections of cultures in ways and amounts unknown to other eras. Western culture, carried by global media, is a potent force and is powered by vast political and economic engines looking for influence and markets. But local culture has its own traditions, strengths, resources, and resistance on which to draw.

Finally, our emphasis on the negotiation of cultural forms at the local level is of theoretical but also of methodological importance. Scholars and writers who wish to write about globalization and culture need to be grounded—literally. Cultures converge not in the abstract but in newsrooms, cabarets, churches, mosques, movie theaters, and living rooms—as well as in chat rooms and McDonald's restaurants.

8

CONCLUSION

The Globalization of False Promises

One summer evening, I was flying over Afghanistan into Pakistan on my way to Singapore. Far below me, I knew, was war. Men and women from the United States and other nations were fighting Afghan rebel forces. Somewhere, across the border in Pakistan, Osama bin Laden still lived and the al-Qaeda terrorist group trained.

I was going to a conference on the potential of mobile phones to transform our world.

"HOMO HOMINI LUPUS"

This book has been a critical exploration of globalization and media. It sometimes has been a difficult book to write. I often wondered why. I think the trouble stemmed from a kind of . . . spiritual struggle. I am usually exceedingly optimistic. I bring this sanguine approach to my work. I tried to bring my optimism to this book. I still have hopes that media can transform our world. Yet I have been regularly disappointed throughout my research.

Globalization and media have done wondrous deeds. They have succeeded in bringing the world closer together. They have removed the shackles of time and space. They have given us the ability to truly imagine the world as a global village. As you know, when McLuhan first conceived the term, he too had optimistic hopes.[1] Even today, the term *global village* still evokes community, kinship, cooperation, and fraternity.

But Lewis Mumford was not fooled. His cold, clear vision of human weakness saw emerging the dark contours of the global village. He saw media technology used not to better the world but to exploit the world in pursuit of property, profit, and power.[2] Globalization and media have

141

fulfilled Mumford's worst fears. They have built a village with large tracts of economic injustice, political repression, and cultural conflict. They have sewn seeds of bitter and deadly discord between nations, classes, political parties, ethnic groups, religions, and neighbors. They have pit humans against nature. They have despoiled the very globe they encircle.

Are these things called "globalization" and "media" really responsible for this global village of Babel? I hope that after reading this book you know the answer. People have created this mess. Men and women, working across borders in the arenas of politics, economics, and culture, have constructed this divided world. Men and women of the media, from smug CEOs to hate-spewing broadcasters, bear their share of responsibility. People suffer not because of some abstraction called "globalization." They suffer because—in a Latin phrase attributed to the Roman playwright Plautus—*homo homini lupus*: "Man is a wolf to man." Sigmund Freud used the phrase as the cornerstone of his great book *Civilization and Its Discontents*. In that book, Freud asks a question pertinent to our own studies: "The fateful question for the human species seems to me to be whether and to what extent their cultural development will succeed in mastering the disturbance of their communal life by the human instinct of aggression and self-destruction."[3] Communal life, a global village, disturbed by human instincts for aggression and self-destruction—Freud seemed to anticipate the dispute between McLuhan and Mumford.

However, admitting human frailty, recognizing the lust for power and profit, sharing Freud's knowledge of the human instincts for aggression and self-destruction, I think we can still find cause for hope. Why? Other people.

ROSHANEH ZAFAR: MEDIA, MICROFINANCE, AND WOMEN

Roshaneh Zafar, the daughter of a wealthy Pakistani couple, studied at the Wharton School for business at the University of Pennsylvania and then earned a graduate degree in international development economics from Yale.[4] With this background and education, Zafar could have found highly profitable work in international finance. Instead, she says, she wanted to save the world. She joined the World Bank. "I didn't want to create wealth for people who were already wealthy," she says.[5]

However, she soon became discouraged. She found that the policies of the World Bank seldom found success at the grassroots level. "I wondered what we were doing wrong," she says. "We had megamillion-dollar projects, but the money never got down to the villages."[6] Then, in 1993, Zafar was seated at a dinner next to Muhammad Yunus. He was founder of the Grameen Bank, which provides small loans and financial services to low-income people so they can start or maintain a business. Yunus later won the Nobel Prize for his work with these microfinance institutions (MFIs). Yunus and Zafar started talking. The conversation changed Zafar's life.[7]

"I came up with the idea of following in Yunus' footsteps to start an MFI in Pakistan," she says. "We discovered the 'missing middle' of the micro finance market and focused on filling this gap in the country."[8] The missing middle was women. Zafar started a microfinance program, Kashf—"Miracle"—to make loans to poor women. "Seeing the potential in empowering poor women so they can become economically self reliant and overcome poverty barriers has been my inspiration behind starting Kashf," she says.[9]

The difficulties were enormous. Pakistani culture discouraged women from working outside the home. The few women who would even agree to take the loans had troubles succeeding and defaulted. Zafar fine-tuned her plan. She came up with the idea of loaning to groups of women. The women would help select who would be in the group and receive loans. They gave each other support. They were responsible for one another. Kashf started to find success. Women began mounting small businesses in embroidery, hairstyling, sewing, jewelry, carpentry, and other areas.

Cell phones provided technical support. Kashf employees stayed in touch with clients, sometimes on a daily basis. The organization shared financial education, information, and ideas through phone calls and text messages. The women traded ideas with each other and Kashf. The World Bank points out that the cell phone has made possible microfinance institutions such as Kashf. "The bottleneck in delivering microfinance services such as savings accounts, money transfers, and loans to poor people has been the cost of 'making tiny little transactions in sometimes rural areas' using traditional banking practices," a report noted. "Cell phones and other technology can cut the cost of such transactions and make widespread microfinance economically feasible."[10]

The communication technology did more than bring financial information to Kashf clients. It also helped bring about a sense of community, which then spread outside of Kashf. The women's small businesses were bringing stability to their families and towns. More and more women, and their families, joined. In 1996, Zafar had fifteen clients. By 2009, she had three hundred thousand.[11] Zafar became an international spokesperson advocating microfinance for women. At the 2010 Presidential

Entrepreneurship Summit, President Barack Obama singled out Zafar for her work with the poor women of Pakistan. "Helping poor women has a ripple effect throughout society," Zafar says. "When they make money, they spend it on health for their children and themselves and on children's education. The whole society benefits."[12]

CELL PHONES: A BETTER WORLD?

When I arrived in Singapore that summer, after flying over Afghanistan and Pakistan, I gathered with more than fifty colleagues from over thirty nations in the National Library of Singapore to talk about the potential for mobile phone technology to make a better world. Singapore was a likely place for the conference. The "penetration rate" of cell phones in Singapore—the percentage of owners—is nearing 200 percent, that is, two phones for every person. The scholar who offered this statistic excitedly pulled out his three phones: a Blackberry for work, an iPhone for applications, and a third phone on which to try out applications for less developed phones.

Though Singapore is an extreme example, mobile phone statistics around the world tell an astounding story. In just a few short years, cell phones have become the most popular and powerful communication technology in the world—by far. And millions of new users are added each year, mostly in developing nations. In villages throughout Africa, South America, and Asia—places that may have one or two television stations, no telephones, and no computers—almost everyone has a cell phone or access to a phone. These villages have completely bypassed the West's route to the cell phone—landline phones, radio, television, cable, and computers—and jumped right to the cell phone. In fact, many people are surprised to learn that the most wireless continent in the world is Africa. The penetration rate of cell phones in Africa is 55 percent and increasing every year.[13]

Why is this reason for hope? Our talks in Singapore focused on the applications of mobile phones. In the West, applications—or apps—are often fun or useful pieces of software, such as maps, games, and music. Singaporeans, for example, use their many phones for a variety of purposes, such as to monitor traffic, chart the number of available spaces in parking garages, reserve taxis, watch TV, make movie reservations, check webcams to see which emergency rooms are not crowded, compare prices of goods and properties, buy food—and sometimes even to talk.

Around the world, applications are more basic—and deadly serious business. Just as women in Pakistan use their cell phones to manage businesses, other people too employ cell phones in creative and instructive ways. Cell phones are being used to fight poverty, pay bills, find employment, increase development, and enhance health. In China, for example, more than one hundred million migrant city workers own phones; they send funds over the phones and stay in touch with families left behind in farms and villages. In India, women in the poorest rural areas use the phones for health information and for finding work. Others learn English through text messaging and automated voice response. In Latin America, informal job markets are coordinated and communicated.

Perhaps nowhere, though, is the impact greater than in Africa. Throughout the continent, people are using basic cell phones to connect to the twenty-first century. Writing in *Foreign Policy*, Dayo Olopade notes,

> The best-kept secret about Africa in the last decade is the continent's rapid and creative adoption of modern technology. African countries have for the most part leapfrogged the technologies of the late 20th century to adopt those of the early 21st en masse. There are now 10 times as many cell phones as land lines in sub-Saharan Africa, and since 2004, the region's year-over-year growth has been the highest in the world. When Nokia's billionth handset was sold in 2000, it was in Nigeria.[14]

Examples can be found throughout the continent. In Ghana, a network of people charts environmental changes that provide information on weather, soil, and water supplies. In Uganda and Rwanda, farmers keep abreast of commodity prices so they know when and where to bring their crops to markets. In Zimbabwe, workers transfer their paychecks back home electronically so they can avoid being robbed on payday. Other uses are constructed daily.

Jeffrey Sachs, director of the Earth Institute at Columbia University, has called the cell phone the world's single most transformative technology:

> Rural poverty has in the past been defined almost by its isolation. Communities that don't have motor transport, that lack basic roads, electricity—these communities live by themselves in a state of subsistence. Making business in these settings, even getting very basic information about prices of food products in local markets, being able to make a transaction, being able to hire truck services, being able to call for an emergency, has been impossible until the cell phone.[15]

CELL PHONES—AND SLAUGHTER: COLTAN

As a careful reader of this book, you know we cannot fall into the trap of the "technological sublime." The miracle technology of today will be on the trash heap of history tomorrow—or at least at Overstock.com. Furthermore, a billion people still do not even have access to the most basic phone. And we cannot discuss cell phones without considering a stark irony: the minerals and ore that go into the manufacture of cell phones drive the very civil wars that ravage Africa.

Coltan has become one of the most valuable minerals in the world. It is a key component of mobile phones and video game consoles. You likely have coltan in your cell phone. It is mined worldwide, especially in Australia, Brazil, Canada, and China. It is found in abundant supply in the Democratic Republic of Congo (DRC).

But coltan does not enrich the Congo. It leads to misery. Rebel groups inside and outside the Congo battle mercilessly for control of the resource. Farmers are slaughtered or driven off coltan-rich land. Villages are emptied. Children are enslaved. National parks are plundered. Gorillas, the same gorillas chronicled by Diane Fossey in the 1960s, are in danger of extinction as their habitats are destroyed.[16] The largest toll is on the African people. Some aid groups estimate that more than five million may have died from murder, disease, and starvation since 1996—the year cell phone use exploded. That makes it one of the worst conflicts since World War II.[17]

International pressure is sporadic. The ore passes through many hands before it reaches the market. Authorities and corporations often cannot identify which supplies of coltan are from the Congo. Some human rights groups have called for an embargo on coltan from the region. Other groups say an embargo would further impoverish the people.

Global Witness is an organization devoted to monitoring the use and abuse of African resources. Its mission states, "We don't condone a system where seams of minerals in the ground represent extreme riches for the few and a cause of conflict and poverty for the many. And we will not pardon the selective myopia of companies that make millions from trading in diamonds, oil or timber but disregard the impact of that trade on ordinary civilians."[18] Reviewing a decade of resource exploitation in Congo, the group did not spare consumers worldwide: "'The illicit exploitation of natural resources in [Congo], and the accompanying serious human rights abuses, would not have taken place on such a large scale if there had not been customers willing to trade in these resources.' And, of course, Western consumers eager to buy cell phones and other electronic gadgets that are made with the resources from them."[19]

And so, even our enthusiasm over the emancipatory potential of the cell phone must be tempered by the complexity of life in our global village.

FULFILLING THE PROMISE OF GLOBALIZATION— AND MEDIA

I told you in the first chapter about the inspiring work of Ken Banks and his Frontline SMS program that allows nonprofits to communicate with thousands of cell phone subscribers. I've discussed cell phones in the first and last chapter of this book because they serve as important reminders. First, the world's most ubiquitous technology was not even invented thirty years ago. Thirty years from now, new media—that we cannot even conceive—will be invented. Cell phones thus remind us of another important point in considerations of globalization and media. It is not enough to understand the influence of technology. It is also important to understand the power of human agency—people will invent, use, and adapt media, and will work in concert with other people to shape our globe for richer and for poorer. Cell phones are not revolutionizing the world. People are using cell phones to revolutionize the world.

I want to conclude with a phrase I saw often in my research: "the promise of globalization." Many world leaders, government officials, and scholars have recognized the great power and promise of globalization. As we saw in our discussion of metaphor, people look to globalization as a beneficent power, a tide that will "lift all boats," and a force that will make the beauty and prosperity of this world accessible to all.

Our emphasis on media has provided deeper understanding of "the promise of globalization." It is the media that often create and carry the visions of beauty and prosperity offered by globalization. The media help provide our global imaginary. Through print, advertising, television shows, film, blogs, new media, and other forms, the media offer us visions of a world that can be. For some people, these are indeed visions of the world's beauty and riches for which they strive. For other people, these are simple visions of clean water and working sewers, of adequate schools and plentiful hospitals, of liberated women and healthy children who survive into adulthood.

Yet we must always keep in mind that the mediated visions of the promise of globalization can turn out to be sources of pain, rage, and frustration. They show a world out of reach for too many people. They are a cruel tease of what life can be. They are *the globalization of false promises.* The media's visions of the world have outstripped our economic, political, and cultural ability to construct that world. In developing countries, a billion people still live in miserable poverty. In developed countries, some people attain obscene wealth while others find themselves without work. The reality is that globalization and media have created a global village of Babel. The French economist Daniel Cohen arrived at a similar conclusion:

> Today's globalization is radically different from its predecessors on one essential point: It is difficult to be an actor but easy to be a spectator. The new global economy creates an unprecedented rupture between the expectations to which it gives birth and the reality it brings about. Never before have means of communication—the media—created such a global consciousness; never have the economic forces been so far behind this new awareness. For the majority of the poor inhabitants of our planet, globalization is only a fleeting image. What we too often ignore, however, is how strong this image is, how pregnant with promises yet to be fulfilled.[20]

It is a lovely line: "globalization as a fleeting image." Cohen adds another penetrating thought. "The principal problem with globalization today," he says, "is not that it sharpens religious conflicts or class struggles; it is that *globalization does not keep its promises.*"[21] It is a worthy conclusion. The men and women who work across the varied arenas of globalization and media—from the World Bank to the local news—must find ways to fulfill the promise of the global village.

NOTES

CHAPTER 1: INTRODUCTION

1. David D. Kirkpatrick and Jennifer Preston, "Google Executive Who Was Jailed Said He Was Part of Facebook Campaign in Egypt," *New York Times*, February 7, 2011, http://www.nytimes.com/2011/02/08/world/middleeast/08google.html?scp=5&sq=wael%20ghonim&st=cse.

2. Fouad Ajami, "Egypt's 'Heroes with No Names,'" *Wall Street Journal*, February 12, 2011, http://online.wsj.com/article/SB1000142405274870413220457613644201992 0256.html?mod=WSJ_Opinion_LEADTop.

3. Ed Husain, "Ghonim Electrified Egypt's Revolution," CNN, February 9, 2011, http://articles.cnn.com/2011-02-09/opinion/husain.ghonim_1_egyptians-egypt-last-week-arab?_s=PM:OPINION; also see Mike Giglio, "The Facebook Freedom Fighter," *Newsweek*, February 21, 2011, 14–17.

4. "Wael Ghonim Addresses Thousands in Tahrir Square—Video," *Guardian*, February 9, 2011, http://www.guardian.co.uk/world/video/2011/feb/09/wael-ghonim-tahrir-square-video.

5. Steve Coll, "The Internet: For Better or for Worse," *New York Review of Books*, April 7, 2011, 20.

6. Mark U. Edwards Jr., *Printing, Propaganda, and Martin Luther* (Minneapolis: Fortress Press, 1994).

7. Diana Childress, *Johannes Gutenberg and the Printing Press* (Minneapolis: Twenty-First Century Books, 2008), 118.

8. "Interview with Mark Edwards Jr.," PBS, http://www.pbs.org/wgbh/pages/frontline/shows/apocalypse/explanation/martinluther.html.

9. "Biography of Oprah Winfrey," Southern Methodist University, http://people.smu.edu/lelder/biography.html; "Oprah Winfrey's Official Biography," Oprah.com, http://www.oprah.com/pressroom/Oprah-Winfreys-Official-Biography.

10. "Oprah 'Most Powerful Celebrity,'" BBC News, June 14, 2007, http://news.bbc.co.uk/2/hi/entertainment/6753847.stm.

11. "Billionaires: #562—Oprah Winfrey," Forbes.com, http://www.forbes.com/lists/2006/10/O0ZT.html.

12. Katherine Zoepf, "Saudi Women Find an Unlikely Role Model: Oprah," *New York Times*, September 18, 2008, http://www.nytimes.com/2008/09/19/world/middleeast/19oprah.html?_r=2&pagewanted=1.

13. "Global Oprah: Celebrity as Transnational Icon," February 25–26, 2011, *Yale University*, http://www.yale.edu/wgss/events/oprah-schedule-abstracts.html.

14. Scott MacLeod, "The Life and Death of Kevin Carter," *Time*, September 12, 1994, 70.

15. Carter was also the subject of an HBO documentary, "The Death of Kevin Carter: Casualty of the Bang Bang Club," HBO documentary, August 17, 2006.

16. Marshall McLuhan, *The Gutenberg Galaxy: The Making of Typographic Man* (London: Routledge and Kegan Paul, 1962), 31.

17. Marshall McLuhan, *Understanding Media: The Extensions of Man* (New York: Signet, 1964), 80.

18. McLuhan himself came to see the shadowed side of his metaphor. Marshall McLuhan, *War and Peace in the Global Village* (New York: McGraw-Hill, 1968).

19. The Babel fish is an intergalactic communication tool in the science-fiction comedy series created by Douglas Adams, *The Hitchhiker's Guide to the Galaxy*.

20. Leslie Gelb, "Necessity, Choice, and Common Sense: A Policy for a Bewildering World," *Foreign Affairs*, May/June 2009, http://www.foreignaffairs.com/articles/64966/leslie-h-gelb/necessity-choice-and-common-sense.

21. "Vision," kiwanja.net, http://www.kiwanja.net/vision.htm.

22. Siena Anstis, "Kiwanja.net: A Revolution in Mobile Phone Technology," Project Diaspora, July 1, 2009, http://projectdiaspora.org/2009/07/01/kiwanja-net-a-revolution-in-mobile-phone-technology/.

23. "2009 Recipient: Lu Guang," W. Eugene Smith Memorial Fund, http://www.smithfund.org/public/winners/; also see David Dunlap and James Estrin, "Showcase: Infernal Landscapes," *New York Times*, October 14, 2009, http://lens.blogs.nytimes.com/tag/lu-guang/.

CHAPTER 2: LANGUAGE AND METAPHOR

1. Rebecca Solnit and David Solnit, *The Battle of the Story of the Battle of Seattle* (Oakland, CA: AK Press, 2009).

2. Thomas Friedman, "Senseless in Seattle," *New York Times*, December 1, 1999, http://www.nytimes.com/1999/12/01/opinion/foreign-affairs-senseless-in-seattle.html?scp=6&sq=senseless+in+seattle+friedman&st=nyt.

3. "Fighting Back against Globalisation," *South China Morning Post*, December 2, 1999, http://www.scmp.com/portal/site/SCMP/.

4. Terhi Rantanen, "Giddens and the 'G'-word: An Interview with Anthony Giddens," *Global Media and Communication* 1, no. 1 (2005): 64.

5. Manfred Steger, *The Rise of the Global Imaginary: Political Ideologies from the French Revolution to the Global War on Terror* (New York: Oxford University Press, 2008), 184.

6. Nayan Chanda, *Bound Together: How Traders, Preachers, Adventurers, and Warriors Shaped Globalization* (New Haven: Yale University Press, 2007), 246.

7. Chanda, *Bound Together*, x (my emphasis).

8. Leah Greenfeld, personal communication.

9. Timothy M. Luke, "Technology as Metaphor: Tropes of Construction, Destruction, and Instruction in Globalization," in *Metaphors of Globalization: Mirrors, Magicians and Mutinies*, ed. Markus Kornprobst, Vincent Pouliot, Nisha Shah, and Ruben Zaiotti (New York: Palgrave Macmillan, 2008), 130–146; Peter J. Taylor, "Izations of the World: Americanization, Modernization and Globalization," in *Demystifying Globalization*, ed. Colin Hay and David Marsh (New York: St. Martin's, 2000), 49–70.

10. Taylor, "Izations," 50.

11. Taylor, "Izations," 51.

12. Taylor, "Izations," 51.

13. "Tony Blair on Globalization," remarks given by British prime minister Tony Blair at the 2005 Labour Party Conference in Brighton, England, on September 27, 2005. *The Globalist*, October 5, 2005, http://www.theglobalist.com/StoryId.aspx?StoryId=4833.

14. "Secretary-General Kofi Annan's Opening Address to the Fifty-Third Annual DPI/NGO Conference," United Nations, August 28, 2000, http://www.un.org/dpi/ngosection/annualconfs/53/sg-address.html.

15. Toni Gabric, "Noam Chomsky Interviewed," *Croatian Feral Tribune*, April 27, 2002, reprinted at ZNet, May 07, 2002, http://www.architectureink.com/2002-06/chomsky4.htm.

16. Naomi Klein, *Fences and Windows: Dispatches from the Front Lines of the Globalization Debate* (New York: Picador, 2002), http://www.naomiklein.org/fences-and-windows/excerpt.

17. Michelle Chihara, "Naomi Klein Gets Global," *Alternet* (blog), September 25, 2002, http://www.alternet.org/story/14175/.

18. Shelton A. Gunaratne, "Globalization: A Non-Western Perspective; the Bias of Social Science/Communication Oligopoly," *Communication, Culture and Critique* 2, no. 1 (March 2009): 60–82.

19. Arjun Appadurai, *Modernity at Large: Cultural Dimensions of Globalization* (Minneapolis: University of Minnesota Press, 1996), 1–11.

20. Robert B. Marks, *The Origins of the Modern World: Fate and Fortune in the Rise of the West* (Lanham, MD: Rowman & Littlefield, 2007), 203.

21. Chanda, *Bound Together*, x–xi.

22. Aristotle, *Poetics*, trans. James Hutton (New York: Norton, 1982), 67.

23. G. R. Boys-Stones, *Metaphor, Allegory, and the Classical Tradition: Ancient Thought and Modern Revisions* (Oxford, UK: Oxford University Press, 2003); Kenneth Burke, *A Rhetoric of Motives* (New York: Prentice-Hall, 1950); Lynne Cameron and Graham

Low, eds., *Researching and Applying Metaphor* (Cambridge, UK: Cambridge University Press, 1999).

24. Paul Ricoeur, *Interpretation Theory: Discourse and the Surplus of Meaning* (Fort Worth: Texas Christian University Press, 1976), 87.

25. George Lakoff and Mark Johnson, *Metaphors We Live By* (Chicago: University of Chicago Press, 1980), 208.

26. Markus Kornprobst, Vincent Pouliot, Nisha Shah, and Ruben Zaiotti, *Metaphors of Globalization: Mirrors, Magicians and Mutinies* (New York: Palgrave Macmillan, 2008).

27. "Tony Blair on Globalization."

28. Ambassador Zhang Yesui, "China and China–US Relations in the Era of Globalization," China Embassy, http://www.china-embassy.org/eng/sghd/t768836.htm.

29. David M. Herszenhorn and Robert Pear, "Michigan Lawmaker Steps Up at Ways and Means," *New York Times*, March 4, 2010, http://www.nytimes.com/2010/03/05/us/politics/05levin.html.

30. "Secretary-General Kofi Annan's Opening Address."

31. Thomas Friedman, *The Lexus and the Olive Tree* (New York: Farrar, Straus & Giroux, 2008), http://www.thomaslfriedman.com/bookshelf/the-lexus-and-the-olive-tree/excerpt-intro (my emphasis).

32. Richard Eder, "Books of the Times: The Global Village Is Here: Resist at Your Peril," *New York Times*, April 26, 1999, http://www.nytimes.com/1999/04/26/books/books-of-the-times-the-global-village-is-here-resist-at-your-peril.html.

33. Richard Owen, "Seven New Deadly Sins: Are You Guilty?" *Times of London*, March 10, 2008, http://www.timesonline.co.uk/tol/comment/faith/article3517050. ece (my emphasis); David Willey, "Fewer Confessions and New Sins," BBC News, March 10, 2008, http://news.bbc.co.uk/2/hi/7287071.stm.

34. Daniel Huber, "Oswald Grübel: 'Globalization Is Unstoppable,'" *Credit Suisse E Magazine*, April 10, 2005, https://emagazine.credit-suisse.com/app/article/index .cfm?fuseaction=OpenArticle&aoid=114606&coid=80839&lang=EN.

35. Gregg Easterbrook, *Sonic Boom: Globalization at Mach Speed* (New York: Random House, 2009), 5.

36. Obama for America, *Change We Can Believe In: Barack Obama's Plan to Renew America's Promise* (New York: Random House, 2008), 245.

37. Ambassador Zha Peixin, "China and Globalization," China Embassy, October 10, 2003, http://www.chinese-embassy.org.uk/eng/dsjh/t27161.htm.

38. Kofi A. Annan, "10 Years After: A Farewell Statement to the General Assembly," United Nations, September 19, 2006, http://www.un.org/News/ossg/sg/stories/statments_search_full.asp?statID=4.

39. Ban Ki-moon, "Plenary Speech at World Economic Forum on 'The Global Compact: Creating Sustainable Markets,' Davos, Switzerland, January 29, 2009," United Nations, http://www.un.org/apps/news/infocus/sgspeeches/search_full .asp?statID=419.

40. "About the International Forum on Globalization," International Forum on Globalization, http://www.ifg.org/about.htm.

41. Robyn Meredith and Suzanne Hoppough, "Why Globalization Is Good," Forbes.com, April 16, 2007, http://www.forbes.com/forbes/2007/0416/064.html.

42. George W. Bush, "Remarks by President George W. Bush to the World Bank," July 17, 2001, http://www.perspectivaciudadana.com/contenido.php?itemid=265; also "Radio Address," July 21, 2001, http://www.presidency.ucsb.edu/ws/index.php?pid=25009.

43. Manuel Castells, *The Rise of the Network Society* (Oxford, UK: Blackwell, 1996).

44. Kenichi Ohmae, *The Borderless World: Power and Strategy in the Interlinked Economy* (New York: HarperCollins, 1999), 122.

45. Thomas Friedman, "It's a Flat World, After All," *New York Times Sunday Magazine*, April 3, 2005, http://www.nytimes.com/2005/04/03/magazine/03DOMINANCE.html.

46. "Despite Observance of Anti-Poverty Day, Huge Populations Still Afflicted," United Nations, Department of Public Information, October, 22, 2009, http://www.un.org/News/Press/docs/2009/gaef3253.doc.htm.

47. "Extended Interview: Brazilian President Luiz Inacio Lula da Silva at the G-20," PBS NewsHour, September 24, 2009, http://www.pbs.org/newshour/bb/latin_america/july-dec09/lulafull_09-24.html.

48. Michael Hardt and Antonio Negri, *Empire* (Cambridge, MA: Harvard University Press, 2000), xi.

49. Hardt and Negri, *Empire*, xv.

50. Arundhati Roy, *An Ordinary Person's Guide to Empire* (New York: South End Press, 2004), 34.

51. Kornprobst et al., *Metaphors of Globalization*, 237.

CHAPTER 3: THE ROLE OF MEDIA IN GLOBALIZATION

1. Thomas Friedman, *The World Is Flat* (New York: Farrar, Straus & Giroux, 2005), 536.

2. Neil Postman, *Technopoly: The Surrender of Culture to Technology* (New York: Vintage, 1993), 69.

3. Nicholas Carr, "Is Google Making Us Stoopid?" *The Atlantic*, June/August 2008, http://www.theatlantic.com/magazine/archive/2008/07/is-google-making-us-stupid/6868/.

4. Nicholas Carr, *The Shallows: What the Internet Is Doing to Our Brains* (New York: Norton, 2010).

5. Lelia Green, *Technoculture: From Alphabet to Cybersex* (Sydney: Allen & Unwin, 2002).

6. Harold Innis, *Empire and Communications* (Toronto: University of Toronto Press, 1950).

7. James Lull, *Media, Communication, Culture: A Global Approach*, 2nd ed. (Cambridge, UK: Polity, 2000).

8. Terhi Rantanen, *The Media and Globalization* (Thousand Oaks, CA: Sage, 2005); also see Terence P. Moran, *Introduction to the History of Communication: Evolutions and Revolutions* (New York: Peter Lang, 2010).

9. Nicholas Ostler, *Empires of the Word: A Language History of the World* (New York: HarperCollins, 2005).

10. Carl Sauer, *Agricultural Origins and Dispersals* (Cambridge, MA: MIT Press, 1952).

11. L. H. Samuelson, *Zululand: Its Traditions, Legends and Customs* (Whitefish, MT: Kessinger Publishing, 2003), 47.

12. Barry B. Powell, *Writing: Theory and History of the Technology of Civilization* (Oxford, UK: Blackwell, 2009).

13. Mitchell Stephens, *A History of News* (New York: Harcourt Brace, 1997), 53.

14. Dard Hunter, *Papermaking: The History and Technique of an Ancient Craft* (New York: Dover, 1947), 48–63; "The Invention of Paper," Robert C. Williams Paper Museum at Georgia Tech University, http://www.ipst.gatech.edu/amp/collection/museum_invention_paper.htm.

15. Elizabeth L. Eisenstein, *The Printing Press as an Agent of Change* (Cambridge, UK: Cambridge University Press, 1979).

16. Elizabeth C. Hanson, *The Information Revolution and World Politics* (Lanham, MD: Rowman & Littlefield, 2008), 14.

17. Eisenstein, *The Printing Press*.

18. Eisenstein, *The Printing Press*, 148.

19. Benedict Anderson, *Imagined Communities: Reflections on the Origin and Spread of Nationalism* (New York: Verso, 1983).

20. James Carey, "Technology and Ideology: The Case of the Telegraph," in *Communication as Culture: Essays on Media and Society* (New York: Routledge, 1992), 157.

21. "ICTs in Africa: Digital Divide to Digital Opportunity," International Telecommunication Union, http://www.itu.int/newsroom/features/ict_africa.html.

22. Michele Hilmes and Jason Loviglio, *Radio Reader: Essays in the Cultural History of Radio* (New York: Routledge, 2002).

23. Robert W. McChesney, *Telecommunications, Mass Media, and Democracy: The Battle for the Control of U.S. Broadcasting, 1928–1935* (New York: Oxford University, 1993).

24. Maria-Soleil Frere, "After the Hate Media: Regulation in the DRC, Burundi and Rwanda," *Global Media and Communication* 5, no. 3 (December 2009): 327–352.

25. Angus Finney, *The International Film Business: A Market Guide beyond Hollywood* (New York: Routledge, 2010); International Filmmakers Institute, http://filmmakersinstitute.com/.

26. Arjun Appadurai, *Modernity at Large: Cultural Dimensions of Globalization* (Minneapolis: University of Minnesota Press, 1996), 1–9.

27. Anthony Giddens, *The Consequences of Modernity* (Oxford, UK: Blackwell, 1990), 63–75.

28. "China Leadership 'Orchestrated Google Hacking,'" BBC News, December 4, 2010, http://www.bbc.co.uk/news/world-asia-pacific-11920616.

29. Charlie Savage, "WikiLeaks Allies Fight Order on Twitter Data," *New York Times*, February 15, 2011, http://www.nytimes.com/2011/02/16/world/16wikileaks.html.

30. "Second Life and Multiverse," Life Church, July 18, 2007, http://swerve .lifechurch.tv/category/second-life/.

CHAPTER 4: "THE RISE OF THE GLOBAL IMAGINARY"

1. "Biographical Data: Eugene A. Cernan," *National Aeronautics and Space Administration*, December 1994, http://www.jsc.nasa.gov/Bios/htmlbios/cernan-ea.html.

2. Arjun Appadurai, *Modernity at Large: Cultural Dimensions of Globalization* (Minneapolis: University of Minnesota Press, 1996), 22.

3. In preparing this chapter, I found that Barbara Strauss had reviewed the same theorists in her own study of the imaginary for *Anthropological Theory*. It is not surprising since these are the scholars regularly cited in the literature on the imaginary. Though Strauss' study focused on anthropological applications, her insights into theorizing of the imaginary were of great interest. Barbara Strauss, "The Imaginary," *Anthropological Theory* 6, no. 3 (2006): 322–344.

4. Jacques Lacan, *The Language of the Self: The Function of Language in Psychoanalysis*, trans. Anthony Wilden (1956; Baltimore, MD: Johns Hopkins University Press, 1968); Jacques Lacan, "The Function and Field of Speech and Language in Psychoanalysis," in *Ecrits: A Selection*, trans. Alan Sheridan (1953; New York: Norton, 1977), 30–113.

5. Lacan, *The Language of the Self*, 29–87.

6. Lacan, "The Function and Field of Speech," 42.

7. Cornelius Castoriadis, *The Imaginary Institution of Society*, trans. Kathleen Blarney (1975; Cambridge, UK: Polity, 1987).

8. Castoriadis, *The Imaginary Institution*, 128–129.

9. Castoriadis, *The Imaginary Institution*, 128.

10. Benedict Anderson, *Imagined Communities: Reflections on the Origin and Spread of Nationalism* (1983; New York: Verso, 1991).

11. Anderson, *Imagined Communities*, 11–12.

12. Anderson, *Imagined Communities*, 6.

13. Anderson, *Imagined Communities*, 52.

14. Anderson, *Imagined Communities*, 46.

15. Charles Taylor, *Modern Social Imaginaries* (Durham, NC: Duke University Press, 2004).

16. Taylor, *Modern Social Imaginaries*, 23.

17. Taylor, *Modern Social Imaginaries*, 24.

18. Castoriadis, *The Imaginary Institution*, 128.

19. Roland Robertson, *Globalization: Social Theory and Global Culture* (Thousand Oaks, CA: Sage, 1992), 8.

20. Anthony Giddens, *The Consequences of Modernity* (Cambridge, UK: Polity, 1990), 64.

21. Appadurai, *Modernity at Large*, 4.

22. Appadurai, *Modernity at Large*, 22.

23. Appadurai, *Modernity at Large*, 7.

24. Appadurai *Modernity at Large*, 22.

25. Manfred Steger, *Globalism: Market Ideology Meets Terrorism*, 2nd ed. (Lanham, MD: Rowman & Littlefield, 2005); Manfred Steger, *The Rise of the Global Imaginary: Political Ideologies from the French Revolution to the Global War on Terror* (New York: Oxford University Press, 2008).

26. Steger, *The Rise of the Global Imaginary*, 10.

27. Steger, *The Rise of the Global Imaginary*, 11.

28. Steger, *The Rise of the Global Imaginary*, 10–11.

29. Steger, *The Rise of the Global Imaginary*, 12.

30. Alexander Stille, "Marshall McLuhan Is Back from the Dustbin of History," *New York Times*, October 14, 2000, A17, A19.

31. Terhi Rantanen, "The Message Is the Medium: An Interview with Manuel Castells," *Global Media and Communication* 1, no. 2 (2005): 135–147, 142.

32. Terhi Rantanen, "Giddens and the 'G'-word: An Interview with Anthony Giddens," *Global Media and Communication* 1, no. 1 (2005): 63–77, 66.

33. Kathleen Dixon, *The Global Village Revisited: Art, Politics, and Television Talk Shows* (Lanham, MD: Rowman & Littlefield, 2009); Paul Levinson, *Digital McLuhan: A Guide to the Information Millennium* (New York: Routledge, 1999); Janine Marchessault, *Marshall McLuhan: Cosmic Media* (Thousand Oaks, CA: Sage, 2005); Donald F. Theall, *The Virtual McLuhan* (Montreal: McGill-Queen's University Press, 2001).

34. Marshall McLuhan, *Understanding Media: The Extensions of Man* (New York: McGraw-Hill, 1964), 23–39; Paul Grosswiler, ed., *Transforming McLuhan: Cultural, Critical and Postmodern Perspectives* (New York: Peter Lang, 2010).

35. McLuhan, *Understanding Media*, 23.

36. McLuhan, *Understanding Media*, 3.

37. Marshall McLuhan, *The Gutenberg Galaxy: The Making of Typographic Man* (London: Routledge and Kegan Paul, 1962), 31; also see Marshall McLuhan, *The Mechanical Bride: Folklore of Industrial Man* (New York: Vanguard, 1951).

38. Eric McLuhan, "The Source of the Term, Global Village," *McLuhan Studies* 2 (2010), http://www.chass.utoronto.ca/mcluhan-studies/mstudies.htm.

39. McLuhan, *Understanding Media*, 80.

40. McLuhan, *Understanding Media*, 80.

41. McLuhan, *Understanding Media*, 80.

42. Marshall McLuhan and Quentin Fiore, *War and Peace in the Global Village: An Inventory of Some of the Current Spastic Situations That Could Be Eliminated by More Feedforward* (New York: Hardwired, 1997).

43. Daniel J. Czitrom, *Media and the American Mind: From Morse to McLuhan* (Chapel Hill: University of North Carolina Press, 1982), 12.

44. Czitrom, *Media and the American Mind*, 12.

45. Thomas Friedman, *The Lexus and the Olive Tree* (New York: Farrar, Straus & Giroux, 1999).

46. Thomas Friedman, *The World Is Flat* (New York: Farrar, Straus & Giroux, 2005), 536.

47. Kenichi Ohmae, *The Borderless World: Power and Strategy in the Interlinked Economy* (New York: HarperCollins, 1999), 99.

48. "The Last Page," *21st Century Manufacturing Technology*, Spring 2010, http://www.capacity-magazine.com/wmspage.cfm?parm1=438.

49. Leo Marx, *The Machine in the Garden: Technology and the Pastoral Idea in America* (1964; New York: Oxford University Press, 2000), 193.

50. James W. Carey and John J. Quirk, "The Mythos of the Electronic Revolution," in *Communication as Culture: Essays on Media and Society*, by James W. Carey, rev. ed. (New York: Routledge, 2009), 87–108, 94.

51. Dixon, *The Global Village Revisited*, 1–26; Susan Douglas, "The Turn Within: The Irony of Technology in a Globalized World," *American Quarterly* 58, no. 3 (2006): 619–638; Marchessault, *Marshall McLuhan*, 202–221.

52. Lewis Mumford, *Conduct of Life* (New York: Harvest/Harcourt Brace Jovanovich, 1951), 236; also see Lewis Mumford, *The Myth of the Machine*, vol. 1, *Technics and Human Development* (New York: Harcourt Brace Jovanovich, 1967).

53. James W. Carey, "The Roots of Modern Media Analysis: Lewis Mumford and Marshall McLuhan," in *James Carey: A Critical Reader*, ed. Eve Stryker Munson and Catherine A. Warren (Minneapolis: University of Minnesota Press, 1997), 34–59.

54. Lewis Mumford, *The Myth of the Machine*, vol. 2, *The Pentagon of Power* (New York: Harcourt Brace Jovanovich, 1970).

55. Mumford, *Pentagon of Power*, 293.

56. Mumford, *Pentagon of Power*, 293.

57. Mumford, *Pentagon of Power*, 294.

58. Mumford, *Pentagon of Power*, 295.

59. Mumford, *Pentagon of Power*, 295.

60. Mumford, *Pentagon of Power*, 296.

61. Mumford, *Pentagon of Power*, 297–298.

62. Appadurai, *Modernity at Large*, 29.

63. Marshall McLuhan and Bruce Powers, *The Global Village: Transformations in World Life and Media in the 21st Century* (New York: Oxford University Press, 1989), 102.

64. McLuhan and Powers, *The Global Village*, 85.

65. McLuhan and Powers, *The Global Village*, 95.

66. McLuhan and Powers, *The Global Village*, 120.

CHAPTER 5: MEDIA AND ECONOMIC GLOBALIZATION

1. Linda J. Smith, *Impact of Birthing Practices on Breastfeeding*, 2nd ed. (Sudbury, MA: Jones and Bartlett, 2010); "The UNICEF Breastfeeding Initiative Exchange," UNICEF, http://www.unicef.org/programme/breastfeeding/.

2. "The State of the World's Children, 1998," UNICEF, http://www.unicef. org/sowc/archive/ENGLISH/The%20State%20of%20the%20World%27s%20 Children%201998.pdf.

3. Paul Collier, *The Bottom Billion: Why the Poorest Countries Are Failing and What Can Be Done about It* (New York: Oxford University Press, 2007).

4. Arthur Miller and Gerald Weales, *The Death of a Salesman* (New York: Viking, 1967), 56.

5. Mark Tungate, *Adland: A Global History of Advertising* (London: Kogan Page, 2007).

6. Aaron Frisch, *Built for Success: The Story of Nike* (Toronto: Creative, 2009); J. B. Strasser and Laurie Becklund, *Swoosh: Unauthorized Story of Nike and the Men Who Played There* (New York: HarperCollins, 1991).

7. Miguel Bustillo, "Nike Looks Beyond 'Swoosh' for Growth," *Wall Street Journal*, May 10, 2010, http://online.wsj.com/article/SB10001424052748703338004575230670692008694.html.

8. Steven Greenhouse, "Pressured, Nike to Help Workers in Honduras," *New York Times*, July 26, 2010, http://www.nytimes.com/2010/07/27/business/global/27nike.html.

9. "Boy Killed for His Nikes," News24 Capetown, January 27, 2005, http://www.news24.com/SouthAfrica/News/Boy-killed-for-his-Nikes-20050127; Isabel Wilkerson, "Challenging Nike, Rights Group Takes a Risky Stand," *New York Times*, August 25, 1990, http://query.nytimes.com/gst/fullpage.html?res=9C0CE2DF173CF936A1575BC0A966958260&scp=2&sq=killed+for+nike&st=cse&pagewanted=all.

10. Timothy Egan, "The Swoon of the Swoosh," *New York Times Magazine*, September 13, 1998, http://www.nytimes.com/1998/09/13/magazine/the-swoon-of-the-swoosh.html.

11. "The Nestle Boycott," Breastfeeding.com, http://www.breastfeeding.com/advocacy/advocacy_boycott.html; Barry Meier, "Mother's Dilemma: A Special Report; in War against AIDS, Battle over Baby Formula Reignites," *New York Times*, June 8, 1997, http://www.nytimes.com/1997/06/08/business/in-war-against-aids-battle-over-baby-formula-reignites.html?scp=12&sq=nestle+boycott&st=nyt.

12. "Food: The Formula Flap (Cont'd)," *Time*, July 12, 1976, http://www.time.com/time/magazine/article/0,9171,914298,00.html.

13. "History of the Campaign," Baby Milk Action, http://www.babymilkaction.org/pages/history.html.

14. "How Breastfeeding Is Undermined," International Baby Food Action Network, http://www.ibfan.org/issue-breaksfeeding.html.

15. "Nestle Boycott Ends," *New York Times*, October 5, 1984, http://www.nytimes.com/1984/10/05/business/nestle-boycott-ends.html?scp=1&sq=nestle%20%20boycott&st=cse.

16. "Boycott of Nestle to Resume," *New York Times*, October 5, 1988, http://www.nytimes.com/1988/10/05/business/boycott-of-nestle-to-resume.html?scp=3&sq=nestle%20%20boycott&st=cse.

17. "History of the Campaign," Baby Milk Action.

18. "History," Nestlé, http://www.nestle.com/AboutUs/History/Pages/History.aspx?pageId=6; "Breastfeeding Is Best," Nestlé, http://www.babymilk.nestle.com/Pages/home.aspx.

19. "Email Nestle over Its Latest Baby Milk Marketing Scam," Baby Milk Action, January 11, 2011, http://info.babymilkaction.org/news/campaignblog260510.

20. Robert W. McChesney, "Global Media, Neoliberalism, and Imperialism," *Monthly Review* 52, no. 10 (March 2001), http://monthlyreview.org/301rwm.htm.

21. Edward S. Herman and Robert W. McChesney, *The Global Media: The New Missionaries of Global Capitalism* (Washington, DC: Cassell, 1997).

22. Ben H. Bagdikian, *The New Media Monopoly* (Boston: Beacon Press, 2004); Herman and McChesney, *The Global Media*.

23. McChesney, "Global Media, Neoliberalism, and Imperialism."

24. Ezekiel Lee Zhiang Yang, "'Halloween 2' Banned!" Cinema Online, September 2, 2009, http://www.cinema.com.my/news/news.aspx?search=2009.halloween2_banned_3527.

25. "Katy Perry Banned," Ahlan Live, http://www.ahlanlive.com/5601-katy-perry-banned.

26. "China Censors Ban 'Brokeback,'" BBC News, January 28, 2006, http://news.bbc.co.uk/2/hi/entertainment/4657052.stm.

27. Chris Matyszczyk, "'Call of Duty: Modern Warfare 2' Banned in Russia," *Cnet*, November 16, 2009, http://news.cnet.com/8301-17852_3-10399131-71.html.

28. Christine L. Ogan, "Communication and Culture," in *Global Communication*, ed. Yahya R. Kamalipour, 2nd ed. (Belmont, CA: Thomson, 2007), 202–208.

29. Thomas L. McPhail, *Global Communication: Theories, Stakeholders, and Trends*, 2nd ed. (Malden, MA: Blackwell, 2006), 60.

30. Jan Nederveen Pieterse, *Globalization & Culture: Global Mélange* (Lanham, MD: Rowman & Littlefield, 2004).

31. Robert McChesney, "The Media System Goes Global," in *International Communication: A Reader*, ed. Daya Kishan Thussu (New York: Routledge, 2010), 204.

32. McChesney, "The Media System Goes Global," 208.

33. Katharine Sarikakis, "Regulating the Consciousness Industry in the European Union: Legitimacy, Identity, and the Changing State," in *Global Communications: Toward a Transcultural Political Economy*, ed. Paula Chakravartty and Yuezhi Zhao (Lanham, MD: Rowman & Littlefield, 2008), 96.

34. Theodor Adorno and Max Horkheimer, *Dialectic of Enlightenment* (Stanford: Stanford University Press, 2002).

35. Jeremy Brecher and Tim Costello, *Global Village or Global Pillage: Economic Reconstruction from the Bottom Up* (Cambridge, MA: South End Press, 1994), 3.

36. Author's personal attendance at UN session.

37. Neal Gabler, *Walt Disney: The Triumph of the American Imagination* (New York: Random House, 2006); "Walt Disney: A Biography," Disney, http://disney.go.com/vault/read/walt/index.html.

38. Gabler, *Walt Disney*.

39. "Company History," Disney, http://corporate.disney.go.com/corporate/complete_history.html.

40. "Factbooks," Disney, http://corporate.disney.go.com/investors/fact_books.html.

41. Belinda Luscombe, "How Disney Builds Stars," *Time*, November 2, 2009, 50–52.

42. Karl Taro Greenfeld, "How Mickey Got His Groove Back," *Condé Nast Portfolio*, May 2008, 126–131, 150.

43. Luscombe, "How Disney Builds Stars," 51–52.

44. Michael Wolff, *The Man Who Owns the News: Inside the Secret World of Rupert Murdoch* (New York: Broadway Books, 2008).

45. Stuart Crainer, *Big Shots: Business the Rupert Murdoch Way* (Oxford, UK: Capstone, 1999).

46. Ronald Grover and Tom Lowry, "Rupert's World," *BusinessWeek*, January 19, 2004, http://www.businessweek.com/print/magazine/content/04_03/b3866001_mz001.htm?chan=mz.

47. James Fallows, "The Age of Murdoch," *The Atlantic*, September 2003, http://www.theatlantic.com/magazine/archive/2003/09/the-age-of-murdoch/2777/.

48. "FBI Probes if Murdoch Empire Hacked 9/11 Victims," CBS News, July 14, 2011, http://www.cbsnews.com/stories/2011/07/14/national/main20079515.shtml.

49. Alan Brinkley, *The Publisher: Henry Luce and His American Century* (New York: Borzoi, 2010).

50. Richard Schickel and George Perry, *You Must Remember This: The Warner Brothers Story* (Philadelphia: Running Press, 2008).

51. "Company History," Warner Bros., http://www.warnerbros.com/#/page=company-info/the_studio/company_history/.

52. Andrew Ross Sorkin and David D. Kirkpatrick, "AOL Time Warner Drops the 'AOL,'" *New York Times*, September 19, 2003, http://www.nytimes.com/2003/09/19/business/aol-time-warner-drops-the-aol.html.

53. Dwayne Winseck and Robert Pike, *Communication and Empire: Media, Markets, and Globalization, 1860–1930* (Raleigh, NC: Duke University Press, 2007).

54. Oliver Boyd-Barrett and Terhi Rantanen, eds., *The Globalization of News* (London: Sage, 1998), 2.

55. Greg Philo, "The Mass Production of Ignorance: News Content and Audience," in *International News in the Twenty-First Century*, ed. Chris Paterson and Annabelle Sreberny (Luton: University of Luton Press, 2004), 199–224.

56. Daya Kishan Thussu, "Media Plenty and the Poverty of News," in *International News in the Twenty-First Century*, ed. Chris Paterson and Annabelle Sreberny (Luton: University of Luton Press, 2004), 47.

57. Jodi Enda, "Retreating from the World," *American Journalism Review*, December/January 2011, http://www.ajr.org/article.asp?id=4985.

58. Enda, "Retreating from the World."

59. William A. Hachten and James F. Scotton, *The World News Prism: Global Information in a Satellite Age*, 7th ed. (Malden, MA: Blackwell, 2007), 129.

60. Thussu, "Media Plenty and the Poverty of News"; Enda, "Retreating from the World"; Philo, "The Mass Production of Ignorance."

61. Shahira Faymy, "How Could So Much Produce So Little? Foreign Affairs Reporting in the Wake of 9/11," in *International Communication in a Global Age*, ed. Guy J. Golan, Thomas J. Johnson, and Wayne Wanta (New York: Routledge, 2010), 147–159.

62. Collier, *The Bottom Billion*, 3.

63. "Editors' Note: Global City," *World Policy Journal*, Winter 2010/Spring 2011, 1.

64. Cindy Evans and Will Stefanov, "Cities at Night: The View from Space," Earth Observatory, NASA, April 22, 2008, http://earthobservatory.nasa.gov/Features/CitiesAtNight/.

65. Rounding out the top ten were Mumbai, New York, Sao Paulo, Delhi, Calcutta, Jakarta, Buenos Aires, and Dhaka. "The World's Largest Cities and Urban Areas, 2006," City Mayors, http://www.citymayors.com/statistics/urban_2006_1.html.

66. "The World's Largest Cities and Urban Areas, 2020," City Mayors, http://www.citymayors.com/statistics/urban_2020_1.html.

67. Doug Saunders, "Arrival Cities," *Foreign Policy*, March 23, 2011, http://www.foreignpolicy.com/articles/2011/03/23/arrival_cities?page=full.

68. Mike Davis, *Planet of Slums* (New York: Verso, 2006), 19.

69. Jason Clay and Bonnie Holcomb, *Politics and the Ethiopian Famine, 1984–1985* (Oxford, UK: Transaction Books, 1986).

70. Bob Smith and Salim Amin, *The Man Who Moved the World: The Life & Work of Mohamed Amin* (London: Spectrum, 1999); "Mo and Me," documentary film, Camerapix, 2006.

71. "Mo and Me."

72. "World Premiere of Band Aid Song" BBC News, November 16, 2004, http://news.bbc.co.uk/1/hi/entertainment/music/4015231.stm.

73. Stephen Holden, "The Pop Life: Artists Join in Effort for Famine Relief," *New York Times*, February 27, 1985, http://www.nytimes.com/1985/02/27/arts/the-pop-life-artists-join-in-effort-for-famine-relief.html?&pagewanted=all.

74. Peter Hillmore, *Live Aid: World Wide Concert Book* (Morris Plains, NJ: Unicorn, 1985).

75. "Mohamed Amin, 53, Camera Eye during the Famine in Ethiopia," *New York Times*, November 26, 1996, http://query.nytimes.com/gst/fullpage.html?res=9906E7DC103DF935A15752C1A960958260&scp=1&sq=mohamed%20amin%20ethiopian%20famine&st=cse; Smith and Amin, *The Man Who Moved the World*.

76. "Capturing Conflict: 'Mo and Me,'" *Frontline Club*, September 2009, http://frontlineclub.com/events/2009/09/capturing-conflict-mo-me.html.

CHAPTER 6: MEDIA AND POLITICAL GLOBALIZATION

1. "851 Journalists Killed since 1992," Committee to Protect Journalists, March 14, 2011, http://cpj.org/killed/. The website title changes regularly as it tallies new killings.

2. "Press Freedom and Safety," International Federation of Journalists, March 14, 2011, http://ifj.org. IFJ numbers differ slightly from CPJ numbers because IFJ also tracks "media workers," such as translators and drivers killed in the line of duty.

3. "545 Journalists Killed with Complete Impunity since 1992," Committee to Protect Journalists, March 14, 2011, http://cpj.org/killed/impunity.php.

4. Roy Greenslade, "Philippines Massacre—27 Journalists Thought to Have Died," *Guardian*, November 27, 2009, http://www.guardian.co.uk/media/greenslade/2009/nov/27/press-freedom-philippines#start-of-comments.

5. Bernard Henri Levy and James X. Mitchell, *Who Killed Daniel Pearl?* (New York: Melville, 2004); Mariane Pearl and Sarah Crichton, *A Mighty Heart: The Brave Life and Death of My Husband, Danny Pearl* (New York: Scribner, 2003).

6. "The Truth Left Behind: Inside the Kidnapping and Murder of Daniel Pearl," *Center for Public Integrity*, July 2002, http://treesaver.publicintegrity.org/daniel_pearl#.

7. Personal interview, March 10, 2009.

8. "Mexico's El Diario Pleads with Drug Cartels," *On the Media: from NPR*, September 24, 2010, http://www.onthemedia.org/transcripts/2010/09/24/01.

9. Charles Bowden, *Murder City: Ciudad Juarez and the Global Economy's New Killing Fields* (New York: Nation Books, 2010).

10. Bowden, *Murder City*.

11. "Self-Censorship, Exile or Certain Death: The Choice Faced by Journalists in Ciudad Juárez," Reporters without Borders, January 22, 2009, http://en.rsf.org/mexico-self-censorship-exile-or-certain-22-01-2009,30074.

12. Ricardo Trotti, "Self-Censorship or Death," *Global Journalist*, April 15, 2010, http://www.globaljournalist.org/stories/2010/04/15/self-censorship-or-death/.

13. Katherine Corcoran, "Mexico Journalists Debate Cartels, Self-Censorship," *Atlanta Journal Constitution*, September 24, 2010, http://www.ajc.com/news/nation-world/mexico-journalists-debate-cartels-619468.html.

14. Corcoran, "Mexico Journalists Debate."

15. See, for example, Babak Bahador, *The CNN Effect in Action: How the News Media Pushed the West toward War in Kosovo* (New York: Palgrave Macmillan, 2007).

16. See, for example, Piers Robinson, *The CNN Effect: The Myth of News Media, Foreign Policy and Intervention* (London: Routledge, 2002).

17. Bill Ristow, "Cash for Coverage: Bribery of Journalists around the World," Center for Media Assistance, September 28, 2010, http://cima.ned.org/publications/research-reports/cash-coverage-bribery-journalists-around-world.

18. See "Bribery and Corruption in African Journalism," special issue, *African Communication Research* 3, no. 3 (December 2010).

19. Edward S. Herman and Noam Chomsky, *Manufacturing Consent: The Political Economy of the Mass Media* (New York: Pantheon, 1988).

20. Herman and Chomsky, *Manufacturing Consent*, 2.

21. Herman and Chomsky, *Manufacturing Consent*, 2.

22. Seth G. Jones, *In the Graveyard of Empires: America's War in Afghanistan* (New York: Norton, 2010).

23. "In the President's Words," *New York Times*, February 27, 2003, A10; "Excerpts from Bush's News Conference on Iraq and Likelihood of War," *New York Times*, March 7, 2003, A12; "Bush's Speech on Iraq: 'Saddam Hussein and His Sons Must Leave,'" *New York Times*, March 18, 2003, A14; "Bush's Speech on the Start of War," *New York Times*, March 20, 2003, A20.

24. Johan Galtung, "On the Role of the Media for World-Wide Security and Peace," in *Peace and Communication*, ed. T. Varis (San Jose, Costa Rica: Editorial Universidad para la Paz, 1986), 249–266; Johan Galtung and Richard Vincent, *Global Glasnost: Toward a New World Information and Communication Order?* (Cresskill, NJ: Hampton Press, 1992); Colleen Roach, ed., *Communication and Culture in War and Peace* (Newbury Park, CA: Sage, 1993).

25. Paul Ricoeur, *The Rule of Metaphor*, trans. R. Czerny (London: Routledge and Kegan Paul, 1978); Paul Ricoeur, "Metaphor and the Central Problem of Hermeneutics," in *Paul Ricoeur: Hermeneutics and the Human Sciences*, ed. J. Thompson (Cambridge, UK: Cambridge University Press, 1981), 165–181; George Lakoff and Mark Johnson, *Metaphors We Live By* (Chicago: University of Chicago Press, 1980); Susan Sontag, *Illness as Metaphor* (New York: Farrar, Straus & Giroux, 1978); Susan Sontag, *AIDS and Its Metaphors* (New York: Farrar, Straus & Giroux, 1989).

26. George Lakoff, "Metaphor and War: The Metaphor System Used to Justify War in the Gulf," University of Oregon, 1991, http://philosophy.uoregon.edu/metaphor/lakoff-l.htm; George Lakoff, "Metaphor and War, Again," *Alternet* (blog), 2003, http://www.alternet.org/story.html?StoryID=15414.

27. Norman Solomon and Reese Erlich, *Target Iraq: What the News Media Didn't Tell You* (New York: Context, 2003); Brian Lowry, "On TV: Will the TV Factory Shape a New War?" *Los Angeles Times*, February 26, 2003, 5–2.

28. In American culture, the countdown is often associated with space rocket and shuttle launches. The aerospace dimension complements the newscast's militaristic use of the countdown metaphor.

29. Quotations are taken from transcripts of *NBC Nightly News*. Dates are provided in the text.

30. Lakoff and Johnson, *Metaphors We Live By*, 158.

31. Sontag, *AIDS and Its Metaphors*, 102.

32. Sontag, *AIDS and Its Metaphors*, 182.

33. Roger Cohen, "Facebook and Arab Dignity," *New York Times*, January 24, 2011, A24.

34. Cohen, "Facebook and Arab Dignity"; Noureddine Miladi, "Tunisia: A Media Led Revolution? Are We Witnessing the Birth of the Second Republic Fueled by Social Media?" Al Jazeera, January 17, 2011, http://english.aljazeera.net/indepth/opinion/2011/01/2011116142317498666.html.

35. Cohen, "Facebook and Arab Dignity."

36. Miladi, "Tunisia."

37. Miladi, "Tunisia."

38. "Report: Internet Usage Transforming News Industry," Pew Internet & American Life Project, March 14, 2011, http://www.pewinternet.org/Media-Mentions/2011/Internet-usage-transforming-news-industry.aspx.

39. Clay Shirky, *Here Comes Everybody: The Power of Organizing without Organizations* (New York: Penguin, 2008).

40. "The World's Fifty Most Powerful Blogs," *Guardian*, March 9, 2008, http://www.guardian.co.uk/technology/2008/mar/09/blogs.

41. "The World's Fifty Most Powerful Blogs."

42. Jared Keller, "Evaluating Iran's Twitter Revolution," *The Atlantic*, June 18, 2010, http://www.theatlantic.com/technology/archive/2010/06/evaluating-irans-twitter-revolution/58337/.

43. Carl Gershman, "The Fourth Wave," *New Republic*, March 14, 2011, http://www.tnr.com/article/world/85143/middle-east-revolt-democratization?page=0,1.

44. Edmund Terence Gomez, *The State of Malaysia: Ethnicity, Equity and Reform* (London: Routledge, 2004).

45. John A. Lent, *Malaysian Mass Media: Historical and Contemporary Perspectives* (Buffalo: State University of New York at Buffalo, 1978).

46. Lent, *Malaysian Mass Media*.

47. Glen Lewis, *Virtual Thailand: The Media and Cultural Politics in Thailand, Malaysia and Singapore* (New York: Routledge, 2006).

48. Francis Loh Kok Wah and Boo Teik Khoo, eds. *Democracy in Malaysia: Discourse and Practices* (Surrey: Curzon Press, 2002).

49. Zaharom Nain and Mustafa K. Anuar. "Ownership and Control of the Malaysian Media," *World Association for Christian Communication*, March 9, 2005, http://www.waccglobal.org/en/19984-media-ownership-and-control/861- Ownership-and-control-of-the-Malaysian-media.html.

50. Barry Wain, *Malaysian Maverick: Mahathir Mohamad in Turbulent Times* (New York: Palgrave Macmillan, 2010).

51. Lewis, *Virtual Thailand*; Wah and Khoo, *Democracy in Malaysia*.

52. Sharon Ling, "The Alternative Media in Malaysia: Their Potential and Limitations," in *Contesting Media Power: Alternative Media in a Networked World*, ed. Nick Couldry and James Curran (New York: Rowman & Littlefield, 2003), 289–301.

53. Ling, "The Alternative Media in Malaysia," 289–295.

54. http://www.malaysia-today.net/.

55. Jeff Ooi, "Advisory to All Blog Commentators," *Jeff Ooi* (blog), http://www.jeffooi.com/2006/08/advisory_to_all_blog_commentat.php.

56. "Malaysia: Multiple Journalists Arrested," *Global Journalist*, Fall 2008, 3–4.

57. Shawn Crispin, "Malaysia's Risk-Takers," Committee to Protect Journalists, October 14, 2008, http://cpj.org/reports/2008/10/malaysia08.php.

58. Ian Buruma, "Letter from Malaysia: Eastern Promises," *New Yorker*, May 18, 2009, 33–38.

59. Ben Bland, "Malaysian Blogger Continues Attacks from His UK Base," *Guardian*, August 9, 2010, http://www.guardian.co.uk/media/2010/aug/09/raja-petra-malaysia-today-blogger.

60. Danny O'Brien, "Six Stories: Online Journalists Killed in 2010," Committee to Protect Journalists, December 17, 2010, http://www.cpj.org/internet/2010/12/online-journalists-killed-in-2010.php; "10 Worst Countries to Be a Blogger," Committee to Protect Journalists, April 30, 2009, http://www.cpj.org/reports/2009/04/10-worst-countries-to-be-a-blogger.php.

CHAPTER 7: MEDIA AND CULTURAL GLOBALIZATION

1. Jytte Klausen, *The Cartoons That Shook the World* (New Haven, CT: Yale University Press, 2009); "Those Danish Cartoons," *New York Times*, February 7, 2006, http://www.nytimes.com/2006/02/07/opinion/07tue2.html.

2. Arjun Appadurai, *Modernity at Large: Cultural Dimensions of Globalization* (Minneapolis: University of Minnesota Press, 1996), 1–8.

3. "Norway: Admission in Bomb Plot against a Danish Newspaper," *New York Times*, September 28, 2010, http://www.nytimes.com/2010/09/29/world/europe/29briefs-NORWAY.html.

4. Ross Douthat, "Not Even in South Park?" *New York Times*, April 25, 2010, http://www.nytimes.com/2010/04/26/opinion/26douthat.html.

5. Klausen, *The Cartoons That Shook the World*.

6. Flemming Rose, "Why I Published Those Cartoons," *Washington Post*, February 19, 2006, http://www.washingtonpost.com/wp-dyn/content/article/2006/02/17/AR2006021702499.html.

7. "Muslim Cartoon Row Timeline," BBC News, February 19, 2006, http://news.bbc.co.uk/2/hi/middle_east/4688602.stm.

8. "Muslim Cartoon Row Timeline."

9. "Cartoon Wars," *Economist*, February 9, 2006, http://www.economist.com/node/5494602?story_id=5494602.

10. "Muslim Cartoon Row Timeline."

11. Jan Nederveen Pieterse, *Globalization and Culture: Global Mélange* (Lanham, MD: Rowman & Littlefield, 2004), 41–58.

12. "José Bové: The Man Who Dismantled a McDonalds," BBC News, April 2, 2002, http://www.bbc.co.uk/dna/h2g2/A706736.

13. Samuel Huntington, "The Clash of Civilizations?" in *Globalization and the Challenges of a New Century*, ed. Patrick O'Meara, Howard D. Mellinger, and Matthew Krain (Bloomington: Indiana University Press, 2000), 3–22.

14. Huntington, "The Clash of Civilizations?" 5.

15. Huntington, "The Clash of Civilizations?" 12.

16. Huntington, "The Clash of Civilizations?" 20–21.

17. Michael Steinberger, "A Head-On Collision of Alien Cultures?" *New York Times*, October 20, 2001, http://www.nytimes.com/2001/10/20/arts/q-a-a-head-on-collision-of-alien-cultures.html?scp=1&sq=a%20head%20on%20collision%20o f%20culture&st=cse.

18. Pieterse, *Globalization and Culture*, 43.

19. Pieterse, *Globalization and Culture*, 44.

20. Arjun Appadurai, *Fear of Small Numbers: An Essay on the Geography of Anger* (Durham, NC: Duke University Press, 2006), 115.

21. Edward Said, "The Clash of Ignorance," *Nation*, October 4, 2001, http://www.thenation.com/article/clash-ignorance.

22. Allan Thompson, ed., *The Media and the Rwanda Genocide* (Ann Arbor, MI: Pluto Press, 2007).

23. "About McDonald's," McDonald's, http://www.aboutmcdonalds.com/mcd.html.

24. George Ritzer, *The McDonaldization of Society*, rev. ed. (Thousand Oaks, CA: Sage, 2004), 1.

25. Ritzer, *The McDonaldization of Society*, 1–23.

26. Benjamin Barber, "Jihad vs. McWorld," *The Atlantic*, March 1992, http://www.theatlantic.com/magazine/archive/1992/03/jihad-vs-mcworld/3882/.

27. Barber, "Jihad vs. McWorld."

28. Benjamin Barber, *Jihad vs. McWorld: Terrorism's Challenge to Democracy* (New York: Random House, 1996).

29. "Benjamin R. Barber, Author, Jihad vs. McWorld: Democracy as an Antidote to Terrorism," *Philanthropy News Digest*, March 20, 2003, http://foundationcenter.org/pnd/newsmakers/nwsmkr.jhtml?id=29100017.

30. Barber, "Jihad vs. McWorld."

31. John Tomlinson, *Cultural Imperialism: A Critical Introduction* (London: Continuum, 1991).

32. John Downing, Ali Mohammadi, and Annabelle Sreberny-Mohammadi, *Questioning the Media: A Critical Introduction*, 2nd ed. (Thousand Oaks, CA: Sage, 1995), 482.

33. Downing et al., *Questioning the Media*, 482.

34. "Call to Preserve Ghanaian Culture," *Ghana Broadcast Corporation*, http://gbcghana.com/index.php?id=1.190136.

35. Sean MacBride, ed., *Many Voices, One World* (Place de Fontenoy, Paris: UNESCO, 1980).

36. Livingston A. White, "Reconsidering Cultural Imperialism Theory," *TBS—Transnational Broadcasting Studies* 6 (Spring/Summer 2001), http://www.tbsjournal.com/Archives/Spring01/white.html.

37. Appadurai, *Fear of Small Numbers*, 4.

38. James L. Watson, ed., *Golden Arches East: McDonald's in East Asia* (Stanford, CA: Stanford University Press, 1997).

39. "KFC and McDonald's: A Model of Blended Culture," *China Daily*, June 1, 2004, http://www.chinadaily.com.cn/english/doc/2004-06/01/content_335488.htm.

40. Shannon Peters Talbott, "Global Localization of the World Market: Case Study of McDonald's in Moscow," *Sociale Wetenschappen*, December 1996, 31–44.

41. Habibul Haque Khondker, "Glocalization as Globalization: Evolution of a Sociological Concept," *Bangladesh e-Journal of Sociology* 1, no. 2 (July 2004), www.bangladeshsociology.org/Habib%20-%20ejournal%20Paper%20Globalization HHK,%20PDF.pdf.

42. Liz Goodch, "A Reality Show Where Islam Is the Biggest Star," *New York Times*, July 28, 2010, http://www.nytimes.com/2010/07/29/world/asia/29imam.html?ref=malaysia.

43. Larissa Diaz and Vanessa Diaz, *Cuban HipHop: Desde el Principio*, film (Chub Productions, 2006).

44. Wim Wenders, *Buena Vista Social Club*, film (Artisan, 1999).

45. "Omara Portuondo—Buena Vista Social Club," PBS, http://www.pbs.org/buenavista/musicians/bios.html.

46. "Omara Portuondo," Nonesuch Records, 2008, http://www.nonesuch.com/artists/omara-portuondo.

47. "Omara Portuondo," SASA Music, 2005, http://www.sasamusic.com/a15_omara_portuondo/artist_bio.htm.

48. "Omara Portuondo," SASA Music.

49. "Omara Portuondo," Nonesuch Records.

50. Robin D. Moore, *Music and Revolution: Cultural Change in Socialist Cuba* (Berkeley, CA: University of California Press, 2006).

51. "Omara Portuondo—Biography," Omara Portuondo, http://www.omaraportuondo.com/main.php?lang=en.

52. "Omara Portuondo," Nonesuch Records.

53. Forum, *People's Daily*, March 16, 2011, http://www.peopleforum.cn/forumdisplay.php?fid=17.

54. Francoise Mengin, ed., *Cyber China: Reshaping National Identities in the Age of Information* (New York: Palgrave Macmillan, 2004).

55. Paula Chakravartty and Yuezhi Zhao, "Introduction: Toward a Transcultural Political Economy of Global Communications," in *Global Communications: Toward a Transcultural Political Economy*, ed. Paula Chakravartty and Yuezhi Zhao (Lanham, MD: Rowman & Littlefield, 2008), 4.

56. Liu Kang, *Globalization and Cultural Trends in China* (Honolulu: University of Hawaii Press, 2004), 130.

57. Jhony Cheung, "Balancing Out Positive Information," Forum, *People's Daily*, February 28, 2011, http://www.peopleforum.cn/forumdisplay.php?fid=17.

58. "Ten Photographs That Changed the World," *Telegraph*, September 8, 2009, http://www.telegraph.co.uk/culture/culturepicturegalleries/6152050/Ten-photographs-that-changed-the-world.html; Pico Iyer, "The Unknown Rebel," *Time*, April 13, 1998, http://www.time.com/time/magazine/article/0,9171,988169,00.html.

59. Patrick Witty, "Behind the Scenes: Tank Man of Tiananmen," *New York Times*, June 3, 2009, http://lens.blogs.nytimes.com/2009/06/03/behind-the-scenes-tank-man-of-tiananmen/.

CHAPTER 8: CONCLUSION

1. Marshall McLuhan, *The Gutenberg Galaxy: The Making of Typographic Man* (London: Routledge and Kegan Paul, 1962), 31.

2. Lewis Mumford, *The Myth of the Machine*, vol. 2, *The Pentagon of Power* (New York: Harcourt Brace Jovanovich, 1970).

3. Sigmund Freud, *Civilization and Its Discontents* (New York: Norton, 1989), 211.

4. "Roshaneh Zafar," *Women's World Banking*, http://www.swwb.org/about/team/roshaneh-zafar.

5. Nicholas Kristof and Sheryl Wudunn, *Half the Sky: Turning Oppression into Opportunity for Women Worldwide* (New York: Knopf, 2009), 188.

6. Kristof and Wudunn, *Half the Sky*, 188.

7. "Pakistan Microfinance," PBS, February 4, 2011, http://www.pbs.org/wnet/religionandethics/episodes/february-4-2011/pakistan-microfinance/8072/.

8. Sarah Khan, "Charity Spotlight: Q&A with Vital Voice Roshaneh Zafar," *Washington Life Magazine*, April 2010, http://www.washingtonlife.com/2010/04/01/charity-spotlight-qa-with-vital-voice-roshaneh-zafar/.

9. Khan, "Charity Spotlight."

10. "Push for High Tech Microfinance Part of a Development Trend," World Bank, January 29, 2007, http://web.worldbank.org/WBSITE/EXTERNAL/NEWS/0,,contentMDK:21198794~pagePK:64257043~piPK:437376~theSitePK:4607,00.html.

11. Kristof and Wudunn, *Half the Sky*, 190.

12. Phillip Kurata, "A New Beginning: U.S. Summit on Entrepreneurship," America.gov, March 22, 2010, http://www.america.gov/st/develop-english/2010/March/20100319163921cpataruk0.1110803.html.

13. Vanessa Gray, "The Un-Wired Continent: Africa's Mobile Success Story," International Telecommunications Unit, 2004, www.itu.int/ITU-D/ict/statistics/at_glance/Africa_EE2006_e.pdf; Chris Tryhorn, "Nice Talking to You . . . Mobile Phone Use Passes Milestone," *Guardian*, March 3, 2009, http://www.guardian.co.uk/technology/2009/mar/03/mobile-phones1.

14. Dayo Olopade, "An African iPhone? There's No App for That," *Foreign Policy*, June 24, 2010, http://www.foreignpolicy.com/articles/2010/06/23/let_africa_have_the_iphone.

15. Cindy Shiner, "Africa: Cell Phones Could Transform North-South Cooperation," *All Africa*, February 16, 2009, http://allafrica.com/stories/200902161504.html.

16. Kristi Essick, "Guns, Money and Cell Phones," *Global Issues*, first published in *The Industry Standard*, June 11, 2001, http://www.globalissues.org/article/442/guns-money-and-cell-phones.

17. Tristan McConnell, "Cell Phone Minerals Fuel Deadly Congo Conflict," *Global Post*, May 30, 2010, http://www.globalpost.com/dispatch/kenya/100118/congo-conflict-minerals-mining.

18. "About Global Witness," Global Witness, http://www.globalwitness.org/about-us.

19. McConnell, "Cell Phone Minerals."

20. Daniel Cohen, *Globalization and Its Enemies*, trans. Jessica B. Becker (Cambridge, MA: MIT Press, 2006), 6.

21. Cohen, *Globalization and Its Enemies*, 165–166.

INDEX

ABOUT THE AUTHOR

Jack Lule is professor and chair of journalism and communication at Lehigh University. He also directs the global studies program. His research interests include globalization and media, international communication, and cultural and critical studies of news. He is the author of the award-winning *Daily News, Eternal Stories: The Mythological Role of Journalism* (2001). Called "a landmark book in the sociology of news," the book argues that ancient myths can be found daily in the language of the news.

He is also the author of more than fifty scholarly articles and book chapters; a frequent contributor to numerous newspapers and periodicals; and has served as a commentator about the news on National Public Radio, BBC, and other media outlets. He is a member of the editorial board of *Journalism and Mass Communication Quarterly* and *Critical Studies in Media Communication*. He has been awarded grants from the New York Times Company Foundation, the National Endowment for the Humanities, and others. He is also the recipient of numerous teaching awards.

A former reporter, he earned his PhD from the University of Georgia and received the Distinguished Alumni Scholar Award from the university's Henry W. Grady College of Journalism and Mass Communication. He has been teaching at Lehigh since 1990.